BADER'S LAST FIGHT

BADER'S LAST FIGHT

AN IN-DEPTH INVESTIGATION OF A GREAT WWII MYSTERY

Andy Saunders

Grub Street · London

Published by
Grub Street
4 Rainham Close
London
SW11 6SS

Copyright © 2007 Grub Street, London
Text copyright © 2007 Andy Saunders

British Library Cataloguing in Publication Data
Saunders, Andy
   Bader's last fight : an in-depth investigation of a great
   WWII mystery
   1. Bader, Douglas, 1910- 1982. World War, 1939-1945 – Aerial
   operations, British 3. World War, 1939-1945 – Aerial
   operations, German 4. Friendly fire (Military science)
   I. Title
   940.5'44941'092

ISBN: 978 1 904943 96 9

Cover design by Lizzie B design

Book design and formatting by:
Roy Platten, Eclipse – roy.eclipse@btopenworld.com

Printed and bound by MPG Ltd, Bodmin, Cornwall

Grub Street only uses
FSC (Forest Stewardship Council) paper for its books.

For my son, Steven James Saunders

And dedicated to the memory of
Sergeant Pilot G C B Chapman 404198
452 Squadron RAAF
Age 28
Killed in Action
Circus 68
9 August 1941

Author's Note

The views expressed in this work are those of the author alone, unless otherwise attributed. No criticism of any person (living or dead) is either intended or implied.

CONTENTS

ACKNOWLEDGEMENTS

A great many friends, colleagues, fellow researchers and others I have met along the path of this project have provided input and assistance with my preparation of this book. Without them my task would have been immeasurably harder. In no particular order of merit I would like to extend my humble thanks to the following:

Winston Ramsey, Norman Franks, Chris Goss, John Foreman, Ruth Bloom, Wing Commander B M E "Bernie" Forward OBE RAF(Rtd), Julius Heger, Simon Raikes, Natalia Dannenberg, Dr Alfred Price, Jessica Cobb, Philip Clark, Jim Allen, Paul Cole, Peter Cornwell, Peter Dimond, David Norman, Simon Parry, Philippa Wheeler, Gareth Jones, Tim Davies, Richard Barnstable, Vince Megicks, Flight Lieutenant Mary Hudson, Georges Goblet, Captain Doug Newman (Canadian Armed Forces), Kim Hemmingway, Liz Watts, Ron Scott, Graham Warner, Eddie Taylor, André Clerbout, John Crossland, Flight Lieutenant Keith Lawrence DFC, Donald Caldwell, Jean-Pierre Duriez, John Davies, Hannah Stuart, Tony Holmes, Alma Bostock, Dr Fiona Gabbert, Jack Misseldine, Andy Barton, Jim Underwood, Keith Dowle, Ray Brebner, Aldon P Ferguson and Steve Brew.

A special thank you is due to my old friend Peter Arnold for his advice on all matters relating to Spitfires and his valuable contribution to this work.

For his assistance on matters relating to the Polish participation during Circus 68 I must thank Wojtek Matusiak – not least of all for ensuring the correct spelling of Polish names!

I must also thank the late General Adolf Galland, Jeff West, Bob Morton and Gerhard Schoepfel.

I would also like to give special thanks to the Battle of Britain pilot Squadron Leader Peter Brown, AFC, who spent a good few hours – and over a long period of time – talking to me about various technical, tactical, strategic and historical issues. Peter, you certainly helped me get a number of things clearer in my head and were a willing pair of ears when it came to talking the various issues through.

Last, but by no means least, I am indebted to the late Squadron Leader L H "Buck" Casson DFC. Without his candour, without his contact with me over many years and without his account to me of events during that fateful day this book would never have been written. RIP, Blue One.

If I have unintentionally forgotten or omitted anyone then I offer my unreserved apologies.

INTRODUCTION

Portrait of Squadron Leader D R S Bader DSO, DFC, by Cuthbert Orde.

Douglas Bader was a legendary if not iconic figure of World War Two. Views about Bader the man, the fighter leader and Bader the pilot have always been polarised and, to an extent, he has been a controversial figure – both during and since the war and, not least of all, through his involvement in the "Big Wing" episode in the history of RAF Fighter Command. This, though, is not a biographical study of the man himself but the examination of an event for which he is arguably most famous – being brought down and taken prisoner of war over France during August 1941. It is a story which has been famously told in his biography *Reach for the Sky*, and in the film of the same name where his part was portrayed by Kenneth More.

There can surely be few who are not already familiar with the dramatic story of his apparent mid-air collision with a Messerschmitt 109 and his desperate life or death struggle to escape by parachute as one of his artificial legs became trapped in the cockpit of his Spitfire. For decades this has been accepted as an accurate version of events that day and it is only in recent years that a question mark has been placed over what really happened. This book, then, is a thorough examination of events that day and the contents may be considered by some to be controversial in that the widely accepted "official" version of events is questioned, challenged and refuted. The author, though, does not seek to be revisionist. Instead, it is the intention to present the known and verifiable facts along with more recently discovered details of what took place that day. In addition, to offer up some hard physical evidence and proffer an alternative interpretation as to what transpired in the skies above northern France during Bader's last fight. Notwithstanding the fact that this is not a Bader biography it would, nonetheless, be remiss not to paint a brief thumbnail sketch of Bader the man before moving on with this extraordinary account.

Douglas Robert Steuart Bader was born in St John's Wood, London, on 21 February 1910, the second son of Jessie and Frederick Bader. Shortly after his birth the family re-located to India where Frederick worked as a civil engineer, although it was not long before the young Douglas was returned to the United Kingdom to be looked after by relatives on the Isle of Man. It was not until he was almost two years old that Douglas rejoined the family although, by 1913, they had returned for good to England. Upon the outbreak of war Frederick accepted a commission in the Royal Engineers and served with them in France, being severely wounded in the head during 1917.

Separation from his father thus became a feature of the young Douglas's life, and this was compounded by his later admission to private boarding schools – first at Eastbourne and then at Oxford. From here he won a prize cadetship to the RAF College at Cranwell in 1928, where, in 1930, he was commissioned and posted to 23 Squadron at Kenley, then flying Gamecocks, and eventually to fly at the Hendon Air Display in 1931 as an aerobatic competition pilot. The following year, on 14 December, and still with 23 Squadron, he crashed at Woodley aerodrome after unauthorised aerobatics in a Bristol Bulldog and was seriously injured. As a result, he lost both legs; the right one above the knee and the left below.

Bader was invalided out of the service on 30 April 1933, unfit for flying duties, and obtained employment with the Asiatic Petroleum Company (later Shell) although, prior to the outbreak of war, he had agitated to return to active flying and was finally accepted after a test at the Central Flying School, Upavon, on 18 October 1939. With the rank of flying officer, and after a brief refresher course, he was posted on 7 February 1940 to 19 Squadron at Duxford, flying Spitfires, and then on to 222 Squadron, also at Duxford and also with Spitfires, as flight commander during March.

Bader's career progression was, by any standards, extremely rapid and by early July he was promoted to acting squadron leader and posted to command 242 Squadron flying Hurricanes at Coltishall. It was here during the Battle of Britain that he began to make a name for himself, and although his early wartime career was spent flying the Spitfire it was as a Hurricane pilot that he made the majority of his victory claims. On 18 March of the following year he was again promoted, this time to acting wing commander, and posted to RAF Tangmere as wing commander flying to command the Tangmere Wing and, once more, flying Spitfires.

During the spring and summer of 1941 he had added to his tally of victory claims but, on 9 August, his fighting career came to an abrupt end when he was brought down over northern France and taken prisoner of war. To reiterate, the biographical detail of Douglas Bader's life can be found, well covered, in a variety of other places although it is appropriate to mention here that his retired RAF rank was group captain with DSO and bar and DFC and bar, Légion d'Honneur, Croix de Guerre and a Mention in Dispatches. He was made a CBE for services to disabled people in 1956 and appointed a KBE in 1976 and died suddenly on 5 September 1982.

Note: All times quoted are standardised at BST for both the RAF and Luftwaffe to avoid any confusion with Central European Time then being used by the Germans.

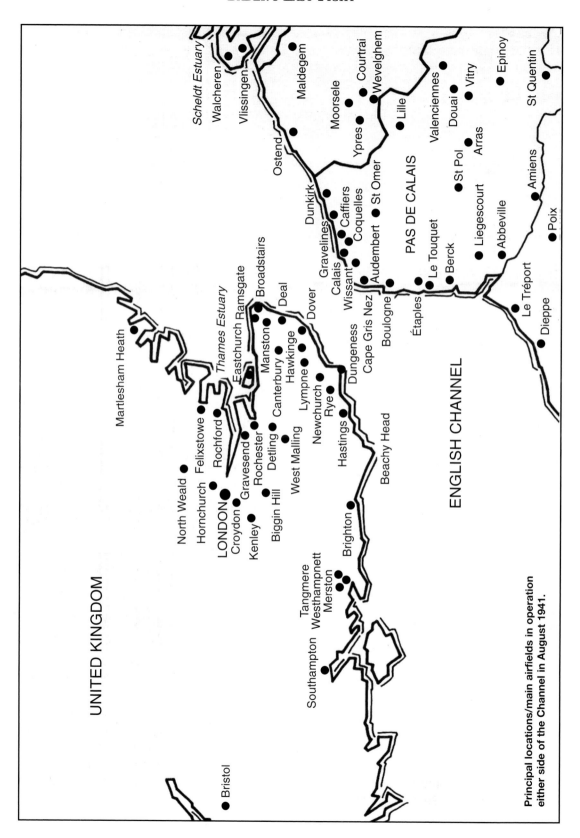

Principal locations/main airfields in operation either side of the Channel in August 1941.

CHAPTER ONE

SETTING THE SCENE

Throughout 1940, both in France and in the British Isles, the role of RAF Fighter Command had been a defensive one but the lessening of daylight attacks on Britain during the latter part of the Battle of Britain and a change of tactics by the Luftwaffe to, primarily, night bombing attacks led to a re-think of Fighter Command's tactics. At the end of 1940 there could not be any real certainty that the daylight offensive which had epitomised the Battle of Britain would not resume once the better weather returned. However, whilst Fighter Command needed to maintain an ever vigilant air defence of the United Kingdom, the air staff had decided to try to seize the initiative and take an offensive stance against the Luftwaffe in north-west Europe. Accordingly, a policy of using fighter-escorted bombers to attack targets – primarily over France – was decided upon with the aim of enticing the Luftwaffe fighter force into action and thereby preventing the renewal of daylight attacks on Britain.

Initially at least, the scheme would also demonstrate the rather more aggressive stance of the newly incoming AOC of 11 Group, RAF Fighter Command, Air-Vice-Marshal Leigh-

Air Vice-Marshal Sir Trafford Leigh-Mallory, AOC 11 Group Fighter Command during 1941. *(via N Franks)*

Mallory. It is no coincidence, perhaps, that Bader was soon to be appointed wing commander flying to lead the very cutting edge of 11 Group in the form of the Tangmere Wing which would ultimately play a key role in the new operations. Bader was very much a "Leigh-Mallory man", having been implicated in the "Big Wing" controversy of the previous summer when 12 Group, of which Leigh-Mallory was then AOC, instigated the use of "Big Wings" to confront German attacks.

Bader's loyalty to his then AOC, and his undoubtedly bullish and forceful spirit, as well as his perceived leadership skills, made him an obvious choice for a key posting within Leigh-Mallory's command. In addition to Leigh-Mallory's clear desire to stamp his mark on 11 Group operations, the new AOC of 2 Group (the Bomber Command Group undertaking the sharp-end of the recently conceived offensive), Air Vice-Marshal Donald Stevenson, also had a steely desire to advance his own career. Incidentally, it could be argued that the plans now being conceived would promote Stevenson's ambitious desire, and there was certainly a view amongst some of the 2 Group aircrews that he put personal glory ahead of anything else. Nevertheless, the directions for the two group commanders came straight from the air staff.

Originally the plan, codenamed Circus, had been that the new offensive strategy would be put into operation during December 1940. In the event, however, bad weather prevented the combined forces of RAF Bomber and Fighter Command seeing any action until the new year. Thus it was on 10 January 1941 that operations finally began.

The operational order for Circus 1 was clear, and reflected the initiation of a new and enduring phase of the air war. It read:

Intention; To harass the enemy on the ground by bombing Forêt de Guînes and destroy enemy aircraft in the air, or, should none be seen, to ground strafe St Inglevert aerodrome.

The scene was set.

As it transpired, Circus 1 was not exactly an outstanding success. Six Blenheims of 114 Squadron bombed an ammunition dump in the Forêt de Guînes, escorted by no less than seventy-two fighters from 11 Group. A few hits on the target were observed but the Luftwaffe had not joined the fight as had been hoped. A pinprick had been inflicted upon the enemy, who had engaged the fringes of the fighter escort and taken out Pilot Officer William McConnell of 249 Squadron. McConnell, wounded in the thigh, baled out into the sea whilst his Hurricane, P3579, flew headlong into the white cliffs at Dover. Wounded and out of the fray for months, McConnell became the first RAF casualty of Circus operations. For its part, the RAF lost none of the bomber force and claimed as destroyed two Luftwaffe fighters. Quite likely, the initial effect upon morale for the RAF fighter pilots would have been positive after long months of being on the receiving end, although that would change as losses mounted and pilots began to question the value of the operations to which they had been committed. In the bigger picture, though, it is interesting to note the Luftwaffe response which was to continue the night blitz against Britain; during the night previous to Circus 1, a massive assault had been launched against Manchester and a secondary attack on London. The following night a major attack was carried out against Portsmouth. Damage and casualties were severe, although the attacking force suffered no losses to British defences.

Slowly, the Circus operations gained momentum although any ongoing success was minimal. The targets attacked were, by and large, fairly inconsequential in terms of their overall importance to the German war effort. Power stations, distilleries and other factory locations perhaps were affecting the French civilian population more than the occupying Germans. Certainly, French civilians were dying as a result of attention from their allies and French commercial interests were being harmed. Recognising that these attacks were a nuisance more than anything else, the Luftwaffe often refused to be drawn into combat and chose instead to do battle on its own terms when it could seize the advantage. This was not, of course, quite how the air staff had intended these Circus operations to be. They had set out very clearly their objective:

> The object of these attacks is to force the enemy to give battle under conditions tactically favourable to our fighters. In order to compel him to do so, the bombers must cause sufficient damage to make it impossible for him to ignore them or refuse to fight on our terms.

Unfortunately, the small force of bombers usually employed, together with the choice of target and the limited damage often caused, did not exactly encourage the Luftwaffe to play the game according to the desires and wishes of the air ministry!

All of this is not to say, however, that the Luftwaffe fighter force stayed permanently at home. In any event, their own airfields were sometimes the subject of attack and therefore the fighter force became increasingly compelled to come up and fight. Certainly, it was no picnic for RAF Fighter Command as the mounting losses began to testify – although the intention to use these Circus operations to deny the Luftwaffe the opportunity to resume its daylight attacks was, as it turned out, somewhat misplaced. The German high command now had ambitions towards the east which, in any event, precluded any further meaningful assault, aerial or otherwise, against the British Isles.

In any case, after its daylight losses during the summer of 1940, the Luftwaffe preferred instead to send its attacking forces by night. Whilst not impotent, the British night defence capability was far from its full potential. True, the anti-aircraft artillery was pretty formidable and the night fighter force was certainly not to be dismissed – but the bombers' attrition rate was hugely less than that which had been suffered by day. What the continued Circus missions did achieve, though, was to tie up a substantial German defensive fighter force on the Channel coast which might otherwise have been deployed on the as yet unopened eastern front. That said, it is surely unthinkable that the Luftwaffe high command would have denuded the north-western European front of an effective fighter defence force – regardless of whether or not the RAF embarked upon Circus operations and other harrying attacks.

Circus missions, though, were not the only tactic in Fighter Command's newly found offensive role. Since December 1940 occasional sorties called Rhubarbs were being flown by pairs of RAF fighters over the enemy coast. These short-range daytime raids, often under cover of cloud, were also designed to draw a Luftwaffe reaction and tie up the fighter force. But, as with the Circus missions, they did not always lure the Luftwaffe as intended.

As the spring of 1941 approached, however, the tempo of the Circuses increased and there is little doubt that this suited Bader's aggressive nature. Ultimately, though, it would be his undoing and with the RAF now trying to take the air war to the Luftwaffe the situation being faced by British pilots was exactly that being faced by the Germans during the Battle of Britain. In other words, large fighter forces tied to bomber defence and facing a two-way channel crossing with a high probability of combat along the way. Should they be unfortunate enough to be shot down over enemy territory but survive, then being taken prisoner was an almost inevitable consequence. As such, they were as much a "loss" to their own side as they were if they had been killed. Equally, should the enemy decide to come and fight it would almost always be on his terms. In other words, as the Circus missions milled around and formed up, the Luftwaffe usually had ample time to climb and position itself for attack. Very often, the Luftwaffe pilots would pick off stragglers, those on the outer fringes of the formations, or else wait for the coastal flak to disrupt the formations and then pounce on targets that were advantageous for them. Usually, and often fatally for the RAF fighter pilots, the German fighter pilots would already be both up-sun *and* up higher.

While RAF Fighter Command was not without its core of experienced and combat-bloodied pilots many were relatively green. On the opposing side, the Luftwaffe fighter arm presented a skilled and professional force, well equipped with the new Messerschmitt 109 F, and well led. Again, though, there was inevitably a percentage of new pilots who had yet to see action. It was against this background, and with only half a dozen Circus operations yet flown by the RAF, that Wing Commander Douglas Bader took up his new appointment as OC the Tangmere Wing, comprising 145, 610 and 616 Squadrons – all operating Spitfires.

Bader sits centre stage with all his pilots of the Tangmere Wing, Westhampnett, 7 August 1941 – the very day that the fateful operational order for Circus 68 was being drafted. *(Jeff West)*

At his West Sussex base, Bader wasted no time in licking the wing into shape whilst the tempo of cross-channel operations increased. This was partly achieved by substituting existing pilots and the officer cadre (and not just pilots) with men admiring of, and agreeable to, Bader. Within a short time he had replaced existing squadron and flight commanders with such men. 610 Squadron lost Squadron Leader Ellis and Flight Lieutenants Pegge and Norris for Squadron Leader Ken Holden and Flight Lieutenants Crowley-Milling and Lee Knight. From 145 Squadron went its CO, Squadron Leader Leather, replaced by Squadron Leader Stan Turner.

In a sense, it would eventually become a baptism of fire for the wing – especially into June and July as Circuses, Rhubarbs and fighter sweeps were regularly flown by the pilots from Tangmere. Inevitably, the losses rose as the tally of operations flown increased. The figures across Circus-participating fighter squadrons, onwards from Circus 1 and into mid-July, are shown as 122 pilots (killed and prisoner) and 161 fighters. These numbers are extrapolated from the No 11 Group operations record book (appendices) and although they present a heavy toll the *actual* figure would seem to be much higher. Even the most rudimentary of tallies, squadron by squadron, throws up a figure in excess of 200 pilots killed and over seventy-five as prisoners of war for the corresponding period. Incredibly, on the credit side

A frequently seen image of Bader as Tangmere wing leader in the cockpit of his Spitfire during the early summer of 1941. The wing commander's official pennant can be seen below and forward of the front canopy screen. *(via N Franks)*

the RAF was *claiming* 311 enemy aircraft destroyed, 130 probably destroyed and 159 damaged for the same period. Primarily, these claims related to fighter aircraft. As an approximation, the Luftwaffe order of battle as at January 1941 shows something in the region of 610 fighter aircraft on strength across the whole of Norway, Holland, Belgium and France. If the RAF claims were accurate, therefore, a full half of the Luftwaffe's entire fighter strength had been wiped out by 14 July 1941 during Circus and other offensive operations. Not only that, but fifty percent of the surviving aircraft had probably been destroyed and the remainder damaged. An impressive tally indeed. Against figures like that it may look as if the Circus missions were worth the high cost to the RAF.

The reality, though, was somewhat different. The Luftwaffe was not being clawed out of the sky in such numbers and the RAF was losing significantly more fighter aircraft and pilots than was comfortable. As we shall see, the incidence of over-claiming by RAF Fighter Command is very well illustrated on the day which concerns the very subject of this book. By late July 1941 RAF Bomber Command's official assessment of the Circus operations was clear:

> The Germans are defending against the bombers, but are not interested in engaging fighters on their own. The Circus operations are not really very successful and bombing France will not empty Germany of fighters.

The same document went on to express the view that bombing France, especially her industrial targets, would foment internal trouble for the Germans and maybe even lead to a revolt from French workers, especially where the communists had influence. The Pas de

Calais and Lille area, it said, was especially sensitive. It was, though, a rather forlorn hope.

Indeed, during August, Bomber Command was being a little more forthright in its criticism of Circuses:

> British casualties have worsened during August probably because the German warning system has improved and they are combining their training schools for more pilots and these pilots learn quite quickly from experience, i.e. the new pilots are not coming in from the east. In addition, German tactics are improving. If there are just a few fighters and bombers the German 'planes wait for flak to divide them and then attack any stragglers. This way they stand less chance of losing German aircraft. We need to increase the number of bombers to get the Germans to attack en-masse in order to give British fighters a chance of getting at them.

A slightly different viewpoint was being put forward by Fighter Command on 6 August 1941 – just three days prior to Circus 68 during which Bader was downed – when its intelligence summary gave a total of 150 single-engined front-line German fighter aircraft in the Pas de Calais. The summary went on:

> It is thought that more might be done towards tiring the German fighters in the Pas de Calais and Cherbourg areas by making diversions in the timing rather than the direction of our attacks. It is requested therefore that the Circus operations be varied in the following manner: A preliminary sweep, with or without bombers, to draw the opposition followed half an hour later with another attack and later by a further attack. In view of the number of fighters located in these areas this variation in tactics should enable us to obtain superiority in a new and useful form.

It was against this general background, then, that the Tangmere Wing participated in Circus 68 on 9 August 1941, although it will be seen that these recommendations of 6 August were not yet implemented. One can only speculate as to the likely outcome of operations on Circus 68 had such changes been made.

CHAPTER TWO

CIRCUS 68

The operational planning for Circus 68, the mission during which Bader was lost on 9 August 1941, was put into play on 7 August. No 11 Group Operational Order 75 called for five Blenheims of 2 Group to attack the power station at Gosnay (NB: the operations record book for the bomber squadron involved, 266 Squadron, describes the Gosnay target as a chemical works and not the power station) with 11 Group's role to provide an escort wing, escort cover wing and two target support wings. The Tangmere Wing was to be one of the two target support wings (the other being from Kenley) and its role defined thus:

> To clear the road to the target area, also to cover the withdrawal of the bombers and escort wings, one being routed the same direction as the bombers, to arrive over the target three minutes earlier, and the other being given a different route but also arriving three minutes in advance of the bombers.

The die was cast. The leaders of each of the four wings briefed their individual squadron commanders, flight commanders and pilots.

The 2 Group Blenheims tasked for Circus 68 were from 226 Squadron based at Wattisham, (although normally the squadron operated a detached flight at Manston for Circus ops) and its five aircraft detailed for Circus 68 made rendezvous with the escort wing from North Weald at 11.00 hours, over Manston, at 10,000ft. Joining the Blenheims at this altitude were 71 Squadron, with 111 and 222 Squadrons stepped up behind at 12,000 and 13,000ft respectively. Sweeping toward the French coast the formation crossed in at Mardyck at around 11.15, and stuck with the bombers until they reached the estimated position of the target at 11.25 hours. Meanwhile, the escort cover wing (top cover) from Hornchurch had also made the rendezvous above Manston – 403 Squadron at 15,000ft, 603 Squadron at 16,000ft and 611 Squadron at 17,000ft. The target support wing designated to take the same course as the bombers was the Kenley Wing, comprising 452, 602 and 485 Squadrons. Again, the wing made the Manston rendezvous and very soon pulled away in the lead whilst the North Weald

Wg Cdr Tadeusz Rolski who commanded the Polish Northolt Wing and led them on Circus 68. *(via W Matusiak)*

and Hornchurch Wings kept station on the Blenheims. As intended, the Kenley squadrons were to arrive over the target area some three minutes ahead of the bombers and did so with 452 Squadron leading at 20,000ft to the starboard of the formation, 602 behind them at 22,000ft and followed in turn by 485 Squadron off to port at 27,000ft as top cover. Meanwhile, and off to the west, the Tangmere Wing were converging on the phalanx of aeroplanes now advancing on northern France having been allocated the role of second target support wing.

Left to right: Sqn Ldr Thomas, Wg Cdr Stapleton, Plt Off Duncan Smith, Flt Lt Hayter and Plt Off Campbell outside the officers mess at RAF Hornchurch. *(R Smith)*

The Tangmere Wing, comprising 41, 610 and 616 Squadrons (41 Squadron having replaced 145 Squadron in July) departed at just before 10.45 that morning, 610 and 616 from Westhampnett and 41 from Merston. Climbing as they went, the squadrons flew along the south coast – past Littlehampton and Brighton and then on to Beachy Head where the fighters wheeled to the south and out across the English Channel towards France.

Spitfire P8332 ZD-L flew the Circus 68 operation with 222 Squadron in the hands of Sgt Pilot Sharples. P8332 was a presentation Spitfire named "SOEBANG". The named inscription can be seen between the cockpit and engine. *(P Arnold)*

403 "Wolf" Squadron RCAF pictured shortly after Circus 68 but including a number of participating pilots in the back row. Of special interest is the CO, Sqn Ldr Tony Lee-Knight, who actually flew as a flight commander with the Tangmere Wing with 610 Squadron on 9 August 1941 as a flight lieutenant and who crops up in the R/T transmission log. He is fourth from left with uniform and cap in the back row. Others are Plt Off Cyril Wood (2nd from left) Flt Lt Ted Cathels (3rd from left) Flt Lt B E Christmas (5th from left) Plt Off Don Ball (7th from left) Fg Off Don Price (8th from left) and Plt Off L S Ford (9th from left).

As had become customary with the Tangmere Wing, Bader flew with 616 Squadron which crossed in over the enemy coast at Hardelot around 24,000ft and then readied to climb to 26,000ft between St Omer and the target area. Behind them, 610 Squadron crossed in at Le Touquet at 25,000ft and proceeded towards Béthune whilst the new boys, 41 Squadron, having failed to make the rendezvous with the rest of the wing, or to catch up, trailed some twenty miles behind them. Quite how or why they had trailed so badly in the rear is unclear and, in effect, they failed to make any input at all to Circus 68.

Meanwhile, the Luftwaffe were watching and waiting and this time they were up for the fight. Indeed, nearly the entirety of Jagdgeschwader 26, led by Adolf Galland, was ready for the RAF and most had sufficient time to climb and position themselves advantageously against the incoming force of no less than 185 RAF aircraft. The detail of what happened next mainly concerned the Tangmere Wing, and is dealt with in the next chapter. We do, though, need to understand the generalities of the bigger picture so far as Circus 68 and all its participating elements were concerned.

Arriving over the target area, the bombers of 226 Squadron found an almost impenetrable 10/10 cloud cover at around 11.25 and, unable to find Gosnay, they swung about and headed back to the French coast. Here, somewhere around Fort Phillipe near Gravelines, they endeavoured to locate their secondary target (the exact identity of the secondary target

Flt Lt B E Christmas flew Circus 68 in this aircraft, W3436 KH-X. The entire complement of 403 Squadron pilots on that operation were officers with no NCO pilots participating.

is not identified in surviving reports) before finally dropping their bombs. Eight fell harmlessly in an open field near Fort Phillipe, the other twelve bombs fell in the sea. So, in terms of bombing success, Circus 68 had failed totally and miserably. Not only that, but the Messerschmitt 109s of JG 26 were already aggressively engaging the RAF fighter force, and with the exception of the 6th Staffel who were still climbing, the engagement was – as usual – on the Luftwaffe's terms. 71 Squadron reported to have destroyed one Me 109 F as it dived beneath the bombers, whilst 111 Squadron are believed to have made no claims, although it will later be seen that there is some confusion on this particular point. 222 Squadron also fired at the enemy but observed no results.

The Hornchurch escort cover wing, meanwhile, found itself in a mêlée just short of the target when Me 109s flying west made to attack 611 Squadron. As it transpired, the contact passed without loss or claim. It was the same for 603 Squadron who were "nibbled at" from the port side but, again, no losses were sustained or claims made. 403 Squadron, meanwhile, attacked four Me 109s as they dived towards the bombers and claimed one probably destroyed – again without loss. Their charges, the Blenheims, had so far escaped unscathed and, already on their way out over the Channel, would all return safely. It was a different story with the target support wings, though, who took the brunt of the German Jagdflieger's interception.

From the Kenley Wing, 452 Squadron encountered a number of Me 109s which dodged in and out of cloud layers, and, in the series of dogfights that ensued, the squadron claimed as destroyed a total of five Me 109s. On the debit side, they lost three pilots missing and squadron records report that they were also attacked by six Spitfires. It was not clear at the time whether this was a mix-up between the pilots of 452 Squadron or if they were mistakenly attacked by one of the higher squadrons. It seemed more likely that in the confusion of the action some pilots of 452 Squadron were engaged by their fellow squadron members. 602 Squadron, spotting the combat 2,000ft below, sent one section down to investigate.

Adolf Galland talks with other personnel of JG 26, early 1941.

The section followed two Me 109s, firing at them without result. Four other Me 109s then attacked two other sections of 602 Squadron from above and in the resulting combat one Me 109 was probably destroyed and another damaged.

During the action, considerable height had been lost by the squadron who turned for home, exiting the coast at Gravelines. As they were turning for the coast, two Me 109s attacked from above and behind and were engaged by the squadron. One of them was claimed as damaged. Meanwhile, 485 Squadron had a less eventful time although one pilot, separated from the rest on the way out, was attacked three times by an Me 109 from 16,000ft down to 6,000ft although luckily without effect. Crossing the enemy coast at Le Touquet, the operations record book blandly states: "This squadron has nothing to report." It was a different story with the Tangmere Wing, though.

616 Squadron, reaching the coast at Hardelot at 24,000ft, climbed inland towards St Omer to an altitude of 26,000ft. Near the target area, some sixteen to twenty Me 109s were seen climbing up from the west and a section was sent down to attack. A dogfight promptly followed and in the fierce engagement 616 Squadron claimed a total of no less than four Me 109s destroyed

Plt Off "Watercan" Gardner who flew with 611 Squadron on Circus 68 in Spitfire W3515 – just one of the one hundred and eighty-five fighter pilots who took part in that operation. (A Ferguson)

A group shot of 616 Squadron prior to Circus 68 which includes some who flew that day. "Buck" Casson kneels in the front row with the squadron mascot.

and one probably destroyed. Before leaving the coast at Le Touquet, the squadron (which had been operating in sections of four, but in no particular formation) were continually attacked and harassed from above by Me 109s. It is the fortunes and misfortunes of the Tangmere Wing generally, and 616 Squadron specifically, with which the narrative of this book is primarily concerned and in the following chapter the full story of that wing's experiences on Circus 68 is examined in detail.

However, it is important to appreciate the overall picture of the operation that day so far as other participants were concerned. Save to say that two pilots, Wing Commander Douglas Bader and Flight Lieutenant Lionel "Buck" Casson, both failed to return from this mission, the brief annotation in the 11 Group operations record book says nothing more of 616 Squadron's experiences that day. As for 610 Squadron, their engagement was rather less conclusive. Below them, they saw the Me 109s that 616 Squadron had gone down to attack.

Plt Off Jozef Gil (top left), Flt Lt Bronislaw Mickiewicz (top right) and Sgt Eugeniusz Malczewski (above), were all pilots of 315 Squadron who claimed successes during Circus 68. Gil claimed a Messerschmitt 109 probably destroyed, as did Malczewski. Mickiewicz claimed one as definitely destroyed. Clearly, all of these pilots thought they had hit, damaged or else destroyed their quarry and yet none of the claims can be substantiated against any German loss.
(All via W Matusiak)

Spitfire P7613 PK-Z was the aircraft flown by Gil on Circus 68. Here it gets attention from the groundcrew of 315 Squadron at Northolt. *(via W Matusiak)*

Ordered to keep top cover, 610 Squadron maintained station but were about to detach a section to go down to the aid of 616 Squadron when some twenty Me 109s approached from the east and just below them. The section turned to attack them but, as they did so, a further ten Me 109s appeared behind the first twenty and so the section kept above the latter. Before the squadron could engage, though, the enemy aircraft disappeared into cloud. 610 Squadron had now become detached and, retiring from the action, turned for home via Dover while keeping one section above and behind as top cover. The squadron returned safely without claim or loss. 41 Squadron, though, played a somewhat inauspicious part in the whole operation from the very outset.

Climbing hard and fast, the squadron were on the tail of 610 and 616 Squadrons but failed to make the wing rendezvous and therefore proceeded alone to the French coast – arriving over Le Touquet some twenty miles to the rear of the other two squadrons. 41 Squadron did in fact penetrate some thirty miles inland at an altitude of 29,000ft, but so far behind, they played no effective role in the execution of Circus 68. Seeing six Me 109s the squadron suspected a trap and did not follow or attack them, descending instead to 20,000ft and returning to base.

Of the Northolt Wing, three Polish squadrons participated; 306, 308 and 315. The three squadrons left the English coast at Ramsgate and proceeded to St Omer via Dunkirk, with 306 Squadron in line abreast at 26,000ft, 308 Squadron in two vics at 22-23,000ft and 315

222 Squadron at North Weald at around the time of Circus 68. Sqn Ldr Love, who led the squadron on 9 August 1941, addresses the squadron and has his back to the camera.

Squadron in fours at 24-25,000ft. Over the target area, 308 Squadron dived down onto formations of two, three and eight Me 109s around St Omer whilst 315 Squadron, diving on to the same formations, attacked four of the German aircraft claiming one as destroyed and three probably destroyed. During this engagement, the third squadron of the wing, 306, sat at 26,000ft as top cover. Losing contact with the rest of the wing after they had dived to attack the Messerschmitt 109s, 306 Squadron patrolled the line from Calais to Gravelines before turning about and heading home for Northolt.

This then, in very broad outline, was the sequence of events as they unfolded on Circus 68. Back home, the participating wings were able to count their losses and tot up a score. All told, five pilots had failed to come home. As for the enemy, the summary of casualties officially quoted by 11 Group of RAF Fighter Command for this operation showed a healthy tally with no less than eleven Me 109s claimed as destroyed, seven probably destroyed and five damaged. Of the pilots who did not return, two of them, Bader and Casson, would both subsequently claim, post-war, at least three Me 109s between them as destroyed and one probable – thus bringing the total "bag" for 11 Group that day to not less than fourteen. On the face of it – and notwithstanding the loss of a wing leader and a flight commander amongst the casualties – this might almost be considered an acceptable attrition : victory ratio. As we shall see, the reality was rather different.

CHAPTER THREE

THE TANGMERE WING AND CIRCUS 68

Although Bader was flying with 616 Squadron when he led the Tangmere Wing on 9 August 1941, the squadron was, nonetheless, officially led by its commanding officer, Squadron Leader "Billy" Burton. Bader was technically leading the wing, and not 616 Squadron, although it would fall to Burton to submit the first official and circumstantial report regarding the momentous loss of Bader on Circus 68. He wrote:

> Wing Commander Bader took the Tangmere Wing off at 10.38 hours on 9.8.41 for an offensive patrol over northern France. We crossed the French coast at about 25,000ft and proceeded inland. When about thirty miles inland from Hardelot enemy aircraft were sighted below and W/C Bader, followed by 616 Squadron, went down and attacked these, leaving 610 Squadron as top guard.
>
> In the ensuing dogfight I saw one Me 109 shot down out of control. The wing was split into sections of aircraft and engaged continuously by enemy aircraft until withdrawing. I noticed that I heard no R/T orders or conversations from W/C Bader after his first engagement. This was a most unusual occurrence and I feel that whatever may have happened to him occurred in the first dogfight and not later, as no aircraft in the wing saw him after that time and none of his own section contacted him.

The stunned disbelief with which the disappearance of the apparently indestructible Bader was met within the Tangmere Wing, and in RAF Fighter Command generally, is well recorded and the supposed circumstances of his loss are equally well known; i.e. mid-air collision with an Me 109, a struggle to bale out and subsequent captivity. However, in order to examine the detail of those circumstances we need to go back to the starting point of Burton's report; 10.38 hours on Saturday 9 August 1941.

A trio of 616 Squadron pilots who flew on Circus 68. At the right in black overalls is Sqn Ldr Billy Burton, the CO of 616 Squadron. Seated is Cocky Dundas with Nip Heppell standing. *(via Jeff West)*

Shortly after the squadrons departed Westhampnett and Merston, as they climbed along the Sussex coast towards Beachy Head, there was the first hint of trouble when Bader radioed control at Tangmere (callsign Beetle) saying, "This is the most obvious farce I have seen in my life". He was clearly rattled as to the whereabouts of 41 Squadron who had failed to make the rendezvous with 610 and 616 Squadrons. Their failure to be there as top cover for the Tangmere Wing was not a good start and a portent of worse to come. Trailing far behind, they were unable to catch up. First confirmation of this was in radio traffic monitored by the Tangmere VHF/DF station on Beachy

The Tangmere operations room, or Beetle, drawn at the time by a young WAAF, Dorothy Colles. It was from here that Woody Woodhall made his desperate calls to Dogsbody on 9 August 1941 – all of them met with ominous silence.

Head at around 11.02. Calling Squadron Leaders Ken Holden, leading 610 Squadron, and Elmer Gaunce leading 41 Squadron, Bader radioed: "Start getting height as quick as you can now will you." Responding, Holden confirmed the bad news to Bader: "Elmer's not with us". Digesting this piece of information Bader characteristically, and somewhat acidly, called Gaunce: "We're on our way. If you are not with us you'd better decide for yourself whether to come or go back." Transmissions from Gaunce were garbled or otherwise inaudible, and not understood by the rest of the wing, Tangmere or Beachy Head. In the event, Gaunce decided to trail his squadron (callsign Walker) in the wake of the vanguard but, in reality, played no part at all in the remainder of the operation.

Crossing out over the English Channel there was another problem for Bader when his air speed indicator (ASI) went unserviceable. Maintaining an accurate speed was essential if the wing was to appear overhead the target on time, and so by hand signals, Bader instructed Flight Lieutenant Hugh "Cocky" Dundas to take the lead. Bader would take it back again on reaching the target area. Once there, Group Captain "Woody" Woodall at Beetle control called Bader (callsign Dogsbody) to tell him there were two plus enemy aircraft to his east, and a little later that there were now

Gp Capt Alfred Basil Woodhall, RAF Tangmere station commander from April 1941 to January 1942. *(N Franks)*

twenty-plus some five miles off to the east. It was Flight Lieutenant Roy Marples, Blue three in Flight Lieutenant Buck Casson's section, who saw them first. Seconds after 11.12 he called, "There's three coming down astern of us now. I'm keeping an eye on them." Moments later he amended the number of enemy to six, then, a little later, to eleven. Someone, probably Bader, snapped: "Cut out the running commentary and just let us know where they are."

Bader's "Dogsbody" section braced itself for inevitable contact with the enemy; Sergeant Jeff West as Dogsbody two, Flight Lieutenant Hugh Dundas as Dogsbody three and Pilot Officer "Johnnie" Johnson taking up the Dogsbody four slot. Quickly, Bader needed to know where all the players were. Responding to his questioning, Beetle control was able to tell Dogsbody that he was exactly where he should be and so were all of his "friends", i.e. the other elements of Circus 68. In the adrenalin pumping moments that followed, Bader struggled to sight the enemy and, at the same time, tried to make better sense of where all his other key players were. At 11.16 Bader had still not seen the enemy, now closing dangerously, and called Marples again for a clue. Marples replied, "Keep turning left and you'll (see) aircraft at 9 o'clock."

Meanwhile, Ken Holden had taken his

Two of the key players during Circus 68, Plt Off Roy Marples (left) and Flt Lt Lionel Buck Casson of 616 Squadron. Here they enjoy a beer and some relaxation time during a dance at The Dome, Brighton, May 1941.

610 Squadron higher and Bader asked him: "Can you see them, or is that you yourself?" Bader must have been doubting what Marples had seen, but a response from an unknown pilot (possibly Holden) told him: "Look beneath you over the cloud." Exasperated, Bader's response was, "Well, you tell me where to look!" Back came the response: "Underneath Billy's section now." Craning to see underneath the section led by the 616 Squadron CO, Squadron Leader Billy Burton, Bader at last saw them and called "OK. I've got 'em".

Almost at once, the babble of chatter between the pilots became difficult for the Beachy Head station to log properly. However, unidentified calls such as "Aircraft on your right!" and "Look out" came thick and fast and epitomised the confusion of a typical dogfight. At just after 11.20 came the call from Dogsbody to another 616 Squadron aircraft, coded YQ-R, and most probably his number two, New Zealander Sergeant Jeff West. "Stay with me!" called Bader. It was the last transmission anyone heard from Dogsbody.

Jeff West had clear recollections of that momentous day when he "lost" his wing leader. Ordinarily, the number two slot would be filled by Sergeant Alan Smith but he had a bad head cold and was deemed unfit for flying duties by the medical officer and so West was nominated to fill the position instead. In its own way, it was both a privilege and a worry for the young sergeant pilot who regarded the wing commander with a mixture of reverence, awe and fear. Bader had barely ever spoken to West. Indeed, as West later recalled:

We sergeant pilots were regarded as necessary evils, I think. He obviously spoke a hell of a lot in the mess with the officers. But with the sergeants? Never. Anyway, one day we had a wing photo taken at Westhampnett, (*actually on 7 August 1941 – Author*) with Bader centre stage, and afterwards he spoke to us mere sergeants. "Oh, by the way," he said "I've heard that number twos are wet-nursing their number ones but we don't need wet nursing. It's my job to take you where the enemy is and your job to shoot them down. So don't worry about bloody wet nursing us!"

Bader dismounts from Spitfire W3185 at Westhampnett. This aeroplane was only taken onto the strength of 616 Squadron on 28 July 1941 and Bader first flew it on 4 August. In total, and according to his logbook, he flew it only three times – the 4th, 7th and 9th August. This photograph, presumably, must have been taken on either the 4th or 7th. *(via Jeff West)*

As it happened, they would later turn out to be extremely and somewhat prophetically comforting words for West. West continued:

Anyway it was a bit of a mucky sort of day the day we lost Bader. There were about seventeen Me 109s coming up and Douglas said, "Righto chaps, we're going down". Well, the four of us went down – Douglas, me on his left, and Dundas on his right with Johnson to the right of him. We flew in a finger-four pattern. Anyway, I think he was tired and anxious at this stage. I wouldn't have attacked from that height because we were about 5,000ft above them and we were screaming down at full throttle around 450 mph. When we came out (*of the dive*) I was just ready to press the titty and I thought Douglas had picked the same one as I had so thought I'd look for another one. The one on the left pulled up into a screaming turn and I thought, ah, I'll go after him 'cos I had all the speed in the world. The other 109s all turned on

"A" Flight of 616 Squadron earlier in 1941. Back row (l to r) Sgt McCairns, Plt Off "Nip" Hepple, Flt Lt Ken Holden (Flight Commander) Plt Off "Johnnie" Johnson and Sgt Mabbett. Crouching Sgt "Jeff" West (left) and Sgt Brewer. Holden was later promoted to Squadron Leader and posted to Command 610 Squadron in the Tangmere Wing which he led on 9 August 1941.

their backs and dived away and I think Douglas kept following the same 109 down. When I went up I nearly rammed it and I could see the pilot slumped in the cockpit after I had shot at it. I thought, "My God, I've killed some mother's son." Almost at once I was in a spin, and when I came out of it there was nothing in sight. Nothing. Nothing. My compass was like a yo-yo but I knew where England was if the sun was up there so I lost height and put on a lot of speed.

Heading back across the English Channel, West saw below him a 109 being chased by a Spitfire so joined the pursuit, catching them up just as the Messerschmitt went into a climb and its starboard aileron fell away. Closing, West gave the enemy aircraft a good burst before haring back to England hot on the heels of the other Spitfire. On the way, West suddenly realised he had lost Bader. "I thought: Oh my God, I have lost the bloody CO." Thinking he may be in the sea, West flew up and down to look for him but saw nothing. By the time he got back to Westhampnett, everyone else was down. When he landed, everyone crowded around and demanded, "Where's the wing commander?" West, crestfallen, pulled off his sweaty flying helmet and could only mutter, "Oh my God…oh my God. I lost him." At first, he felt an irrational fear that Bader had been his responsibility to protect, and his alone, and that the rest of the wing would think so too. Bader's last words "Stay with me!" were still ringing in West's ears. If anyone shouldn't be coming home it was him, not the CO. Later, of course, when the shock had worn off, West was able to rationalise things rather more and made himself feel a little better by thinking back to just two days earlier when Bader had delivered his admonition to the number twos, telling them it wasn't their job to "wet nurse" their number ones. The palliative effect of recalling Bader's words was, no doubt, somewhat comforting under the prevailing circumstances.

Once Bader had gone down to join combat, a general mêlée had broken out with Blue section of 616 following Bader down in the attack. Leading them was Flight Lieutenant Buck Casson, although Blue section did not follow at once. Holding back a little, Casson then throttled back to keep his section together as the remainder had been left behind in his initial dive. In Dogsbody section, Cocky Dundas could not help but feel uneasy about the Messerschmitts above and kept looking back. Although he knew their tails were covered he had a strong instinct that the enemy were right on their heels. Sure enough, when someone called "Break!" he turned to see Messerschmitt 109s right behind them.

In the heat of battle, and with Casson not immediately behind Bader's section but, in fact, a little way out it is entirely likely that Dundas mistook the descent of Casson's Blue section to be Messerschmitts. Confusion reigned, it seems. Ken Holden's 610 Squadron, who were much higher than 616 Squadron, and climbing higher still, had Me 109s above them and had seen just a few below them. Holden and 610 Squadron certainly did not see Me 109s going down to attack Bader or 616 Squadron and Casson's section had not yet been engaged by the enemy – although Dundas, way out in front, believed that Messerschmitts had closed on Dogsbody section and attacked them. The rest of the squadron followed Bader down in the attack he had initiated, with positive engagements reported by Pilot Officer Heppell (Yellow three) , Pilot Officer Johnson (Dogsbody four) and Flying Officer Marples (Blue three), as well as the hits already described by Sergeant West.

Heppell claimed one Messerschmitt 109 as definitely destroyed. Diving down with the wing leader until they were level with the enemy, Heppell climbed up to his right and saw a Messerschmitt 109 F in front of him. The German fighter appeared to be on the top of a stall turn and Heppell saw a large "6" behind the cross on its fuselage as he closed to almost point-blank range and gave the enemy a long burst. The Messerschmitt immediately went into a very slow gliding turn to the left and Heppell clearly saw the hood fly off and the pilot jumping out of the

Ultimately the top-scoring RAF fighter pilot, Johnnie Johnson flew as a relative greenhorn pilot officer in A Flight of 616 Squadron on Circus 68. Johnson went on to be a wing leader himself and ended the war with thirty-eight confirmed kills. He retired with the rank of Air Vice-Marshal, CB, CBE, DSO & Two Bars, DFC & Bar.

aircraft. With an almost morbid fascination he watched the pilot falling and turning over and over until he dropped into cloud, his parachute still not open. Not unreasonably, and in fact accurately, Heppell judged that the German airman must have certainly been killed.

Pilot Officer Johnnie Johnson, meanwhile, having already claimed a shared kill over another Me 109 with Sergeant West, saw a further Messerschmitt below him and went down to attack, closing from behind and below. Black smoke poured from the engine and it went down steeply. Johnson pushed hard forward on the stick, propelling his Spitfire into a near vertical dive in pursuit. As he did so, his engine spluttered and cut – not caused by battle damage but, instead, the usual result of a Rolls-Royce Merlin carburrettor-fed engine protesting at such manoeuvres. In contrast, with their fuel injected system, the Messerschmitt 109's DB601 engines could easily tolerate being thrown into a sudden vertical dive. Clouds of black smoke pouring from their exhaust manifolds was the usual result, and many RAF fighter pilots mistook Me 109s that had gone into vertical smoke-streaming dives to have been hit and done for. At best, they believed they had probably destroyed them – or at the very least damaged them. Often, neither was the case. It was simply the German pilots taking very effective evasive action which they knew the RAF fighter pilots could not counter.

Putting together what we know now it would certainly seem to be the case that Johnson's quarry that day was simply getting smartly out of the way and nothing more. What we know for sure is that Johnson, once his engine had picked up, continued down in an all-out dive after the Messerschmitt and pulled out, quite violently, at around 4,000ft. Pulling up and turning left, Johnson lost sight of his foe but, on looking around, he spotted burning wreckage on the ground in a field close to a canal. Although he admitted he did not actually see it crash he nevertheless claimed this as his Me 109 confirmed destroyed. In fact, what he had almost certainly seen was the burning wreckage of the Messerschmitt 109 that Heppell had just despatched, the pilot of which had fallen to his death with an unopened parachute. In itself, this is a good example of how over-claiming often occurred through the inevitable confusion of war.

Roy Marples's claim, though, was a little less definite than those of his squadron colleagues. Diving down in the attack as Buck Casson's Blue three he picked out a solitary Messerschmitt that had broken away from its group. Closing down to one hundred and fifty yards, Marples put in a good few bursts and was surprised to see the enemy 'plane carry on its course without taking any evasive action. Marples continued to give his quarry repeated fire, eventually using up all his ammunition, and reaching the conclusion that its pilot must have been dead otherwise he would have evaded Marples's attacks. He did not, though, witness any definite results of his fire and therefore was only able to claim a "probable".

By this stage of the engagement, most of the combatant aircraft were widely dispersed across a large part of the Pas de Calais airspace. The bomber formation, together with its escort, were already well on the way home and it only remained for the Tangmere Wing to extricate itself as best it could from the action. Indeed, realising that the main formation would now be turning for England, Beetle control at Tangmere called Dogsbody one at around 11.28 with a simple instruction. "Withdraw now". There was no response from Bader, and at 11.33 Beetle called again: "Withdraw as soon as you like". Again, no response came from the wing leader. The remainder of the Tangmere Wing, as well as Beetle, recognised the silence as somewhat ominous. Eventually, at 11.35, an unidentified pilot realised their leader was not going to answer and called "We all heard it".

Strewn out across miles of sky the shaken remnants of Bader's wing headed for home. Once there, the three squadrons could really not believe that Bader the indestructible hadn't returned. Certainly, all were shocked although it is fair to say that, secretly, there were many on the wing who were not too unhappy he had gone. Bader certainly had his "inner sanctum", a cadre of pilots who supported all he did. Equally, there were others who did not revere him or his leadership. Many of the groundcrews, for example, regarded him as a bully and there were more than a few pilots – officers and NCOs – who were not over-impressed by him either. One who had his concerns was Squadron Leader Billy Burton who led 616 Squadron in Bader's Tangmere Wing.

In his memoir *Straight And Level*, Air Chief Marshal Sir Kenneth "Bing" Cross, KCB, CBE, DSO, DFC, tells of Burton's later arrival at a posting in the Western Desert where he maintained to Cross that by August 1941 the Tangmere Wing had been in a state of near mutiny brought on by Bader's reckless leadership in his efforts to increase his own score. A former pilot officer on 610 Squadron, Tony Gaze, echoed to this author the feelings on the wing about Bader's "kill chasing" attitude and, sometimes, his rather outlandish leadership. Indeed, Gaze has vivid recollections of one incident which cost the lives of both of 145 Squadron's flight commanders which, he says, was caused directly by Bader's actions in the air. Usually, Bader flew with 616 Squadron although it was on the one occasion that he flew with 145 Squadron (at that time still part of the Tangmere Wing) that tragedy struck:

> The only time he led 145 Squadron, who were based at Merston, he was responsible for causing two aircraft to collide. Instead of taking them back to Merston, which they had anticipated, he led them back towards Westhampnett (his "home") and then broke away downwards to land. This apparently took the following aircraft by surprise and they immediately took avoiding action. In doing so they collided. One rolled over and went straight in, the other went into a flat spin and crashed just behind Westhampnett Mill. Pilot Officer "Dickie" Stoop and I were on the ground at Westhampnett and watched the whole thing.

Gaze went on to express his view that had any lesser mortal committed the same degree of poor airmanship then he would, undoubtedly, have faced court martial and most certainly been removed from the Tangmere Wing. Because it was Bader it was glossed over and quietly forgotten, just becoming one of those misfortunes of war. (This "misfortune of war" witnessed by Gaze and Stoop was, in fact, the collision above Graylingwell Hospital on 21 May 1941 between Flight Lieutenant L W Stevens [in P7493] and Flight Lieutenant D W Owen [P7737] at 6.20pm whilst returning from a patrol.) Episodes such as these hardly endeared Bader to everyone in the squadrons of his wing.

However, whether they loved him or loathed him, all of the pilots on the Tangmere Wing were stunned when he didn't come home on 9 August 1941. 616 Squadron's much liked B Flight commander, Flight Lieutenant Buck Casson, was missing too.

CHAPTER FOUR

REACH FOR THE SKY: MYTH AND REALITY

Paul Brickhill's book, *Reach for the Sky*, has become a classic of its type and is perhaps one of the best known and most widely read accounts of the RAF's World War Two experience. It was, though, of a genre typical of its time. Written in an almost gung-ho fashion the book portrays well the character of Bader himself, but published as it was in 1954 it still reflects the brash propaganda ethos of wartime writings. Certainly, it seems that its author had not yet moved away from that mindset. Indeed, contemporary books like Larry Forrester's biography of Bob Stanford Tuck, *Fly For Your Life*, echo the very same ethos. The titles of these two books alone are redolent with images of Boys Own style action and ripping yarns. In the case of Bader's book it wasn't long before the film-makers saw some potential for this tale of heroic struggle and derring-do.

As the story of Douglas Bader's life, *Reach for the Sky* is perhaps as good as we get although, of course, other biographical accounts have appeared subsequently. It is the account of Bader's experience on Circus 68, though, that interests us. Brickhill recounts what has long been accepted to be the "definitive" version of events when Bader was left behind over France. Although, somewhat surprisingly, it was not the first published account of his demise it did nevertheless very much put the stamp of "approval" on how Bader wished the world to view the episode. Brickhill, himself a former RAF officer, Spitfire pilot and an ex-PoW, obviously had some empathy with the subject – as well as an insight and understanding of much that Bader had endured – and was able to couple this with his journalistic flair and an ability to tell a good tale. That said, there were apparently some fractious moments between Brickhill and Bader.

Brickhill perceived his reputation to be based upon attention to minute detail, and Bader evidently did not take kindly to Brickhill's persistent questioning, to the extent that publication of the book was only saved by the intervention of the publisher, Ian Collins, a golfing partner of Bader's. In the end, the book saw the light of day but not without further rancour as far as Bader was concerned. He felt some resentment that Brickhill did very well out of the book and the film rights while he, Bader, only received a one-off £10,000 payment (approx £200,000 in today's money). This was in fact a very considerable sum for the period, and there was a degree of consolation for him when HM Inland Revenue later agreed to waive Bader's tax liability on the sum.

When the book came out it was almost immediately a best seller, and the following film was an inevitable consequence of that success. Without putting either Brickhill or Bader down in any way it was, perhaps, a post-war version of what wartime RAF pilots in the officers mess might have called "shooting a line"!

There is little in the preamble of chapter 22 to Brickhill's book that adds much to our knowledge of the day's events for the Tangmere Wing from take-off to target area which cannot otherwise be gained from various eyewitness accounts or official records. It does, however, tell of Bader's diving attack on the Messerschmitts, overshooting the first ones in his headlong pursuit and then pulling up to 24,000ft, finding himself alone, and then spotting and attacking more Messerschmitts – one of which he claimed to have set well ablaze. Another, the leader of the group, he then claimed to have damaged with a three second

Flg Off Paul Brickhill, author of *Reach for the Sky*, when he was flying with 92 Squadron in the Western Desert. He was shot down and taken PoW on 17 March 1943.

burst that caused a gushing volume of white smoke and a cascade of debris. One destroyed and one damaged as far as he was concerned. Two fighters, though, were now turning to attack him from the left and Bader broke right. As he did so, it happened:

Something hit him. He felt the impact but the mind was curiously numb and could not assess it. No noise, but something was holding his aeroplane by the tail, pulling it out of his hands and slewing it round. It lurched suddenly and then was pointing straight down, the cockpit floating with dust that had come up from the bottom. He pulled back on the stick but it fell inertly into his stomach like a broken neck. The aeroplane was diving in a steep spiral and confusedly he looked behind to see if anything were following.

First he was surprised, and then terrifyingly shocked to see that the whole of the Spitfire behind the cockpit was missing: fuselage, tail, fin – all gone. Sheared off, he thought vaguely. The second 109 must have run into him and sliced it off with his propeller.

He knew it had happened but hoped desperately and foolishly that he was wrong. Only the little radio mast stuck up behind his head. A corner of his brain saw that the altimeter was unwinding fast from 24,000ft.

Thoughts crowded in. How stupid to be nice and warm in the cockpit and have to start getting out. The floundering mind sought a grip and sharply a gush of panic spurted.

"Christ! Get out!"

"Wait! No oxygen up here!"

Get out! Get out!

Won't be able to soon! Must be doing over 400 already. He tore his helmet and mask off* and yanked the little rubber ball over his head – the hood ripped away and screaming noise battered at him. Out came the harness pin and he gripped the cockpit rim to lever himself up, wondering if he could get out without thrust from the helpless legs. He struggled madly to get his head above the windscreen and suddenly felt he was being sucked out as the tearing wind caught him.

Top half out. He was out! No, something had him by the leg holding him. (The rigid foot of the right leg hooked fast in some vice in the cockpit.) Then the nightmare took his exposed body and beat him and screamed and roared in his ears as the broken fighter dragging him by the leg plunged down and spun and battered him and the wind clawed at his flesh and the cringing sightless eyeballs. It went on and on into confusion, on and on, timeless, witless and helpless, with a little core of thought deep under the blind head fighting for life in the wilderness. It said he had a hand gripping the D-ring of his parachute and mustn't take it off, must grip it because the wind wouldn't let him get it back again, and he mustn't pull it or the wind would split his parachute because they must be doing 500 miles an hour. On and on…till steel and leather snapped.

He was floating, in peace. The noise and buffeting had stopped. Floating upwards? He thought: it is so quiet I must have a rest. I would like to go to sleep.

In a flash the brain cleared and he knew and pulled the D-ring, hearing a crack as the parachute opened. Then he was actually floating. High above the sky was still blue, and right at his feet lay a veil of cloud. He sank into it. That was the cloud at 4,000ft. Cutting it fine! In seconds he dropped easily under it and saw the earth, green and dappled, where the sun struck through. Something flapped in his face and he saw that it was his right trouser leg, split along the seam. High in the split gleamed indecently the white skin of his stump.

The right leg had gone.

How lucky, he thought, to lose one's legs and have detachable ones. Otherwise he would have died a few seconds ago. He looked, but saw no burning wreck below – probably not enough left to burn.

This, then, is the widely known description of Bader's bale out over France. By and large, it was an account that was reflected faithfully in the film of the same name. Producer Daniel M Angel read Brickhill's book and at once recognised its screen potential, buying the film rights for a then astonishing £15,000, and teaming up with Lewis Gilbert to write the screenplay and direct the film. Kenneth More, of course, took the starring role – a part for

* In the 1973 autobiography *Fight For The Sky* Bader's account has changed slightly, saying that the helmet and goggles were "wrenched off his head" by the roaring slipstream, and *not* that he removed them. A significant variation in the story.

which Richard Burton had been widely tipped as favourite. As for the aeroplanes, though, the Spitfires used were somewhat less convincing than More's exceptionally good portrayal of Bader's demeanour, character and even his physical stance. For the purposes of the film, Spitfire XVs (low-backed aeroplanes) were used and thus had to rather inaccurately represent the Mk I, II and V of the period. Generally, the film was well received when it premiered at The Odeon, Leicester Square, on 5 July 1956 in the presence of HRH Prince Philip, The Duke of Edinburgh.

Although Bader stayed away he was reported to be generally pleased with the way the film had turned out. Like the book, the film is a classic of its cinematographic type for the period and it told the tale relatively faithfully – at least, insofar as adherence to the book's storyline was concerned. Its frequent repeats on UK television channels, right up to the present day, mean that the story it relates has probably crept into the British consciousness. There cannot be very many war film or aviation enthusiasts who have not seen it at least once! All of them will surely remember, if asked, the cause of Douglas Bader's demise over France; a collision with a German fighter.

Frank Wootton's well-known painting "Bader Bale-Out" depicting the moments after the alleged mid-air collision with a Messerschmitt 109.

CHAPTER FIVE

COLLISION? OR SHOOT DOWN?

"He was shot down and I am sure of it." These were the words of General Adolf Galland when interviewed by the author in August 1977. Galland had commanded Jagdgeschwader 26 when Bader was brought down, and it was his fighter wing which had engaged Circus 68. As such, he was very much a key player that day. Interestingly, he too had written an account of his experiences as one of Germany's most famous and most decorated World War Two fighter aces. *The First and the Last*, first published in 1953 (one year ahead of Brickhill's book), details events of the engagement on 9 August 1941 and, in a different version of events to Bader, tells how the British pilot was shot down:

Old adversaries, new friends. During 1941 the units commanded by Douglas Bader and Adolf Galland met frequently in combat over northern France. Post-war, both fliers got to know each other well and often met at reunions and seminars. Here they sign copies of *Reach for the Sky* and *The First and the Last* for each other in 1978.

> One of the most successful and famous fighter pilots of the RAF, Wing Commander Douglas Bader, was shot down in a dogfight over the Pas de Calais. It was never confirmed who actually shot him down, but when Bader was captured he particularly wanted to know who it was, and if possible meet his master in the air. He said that for him it was an intolerable idea that possibly he had been shot down by a German NCO. It was not an NCO, but probably one of our able young officers, amongst whom there were some outstanding pilots. I had shot down that day two Spitfires

out of Bader's formation. In order not to offend him, we chose from amongst the successful pilots who had taken part in this flight a fair haired, good-looking flying officer, and introduced him to Bader as his victorious opponent. Bader was pleasantly surprised and shook his hand warmly. He described his crash like this: "I saw pieces flying off my crate. The nose dipped, and when I looked round the tail unit had practically gone…Nothing else to do but to get out as quickly as possible."

The extract goes on with a broadly similar description of the struggle to exit the stricken Spitfire to that which appears in *Reach for the Sky*. Clearly, though, the account of the shoot down is completely at odds with what Bader would later recount. Galland, though, was emphatic – both in his book and later when interviewed in 1977. Another who was convinced that Bader had been shot down was Johnnie Johnson who had been flying with 616 Squadron that day. Interviewed by journalist John Crossland in 1989 he told him:

The First
and the Last

To the Great Douglas
always yours
Dolfo
2a Febr. 1978

The frontispiece in Galland's book **The First and the Last** which he signed and dedicated to Bader at that 1978 meeting.

"Douggie was shot down, that's for sure. Trouble was, he hated the idea that anyone shot him down. Absolutely bloody hated it."

That day, 9 August 1941, had seen elements of Galland's JG 26 ordered into the air across north-east France and this included the Stabsschwarm and all of the three Gruppen. The "alarmstart" was shortly after 11.00 when the first reports of Circus 68 forming up over England were received. The other fighter unit in the region, JG 2, remained on the ground although they did fly into action much later in the day when they claimed a Bristol Blenheim destroyed. (In fact no British losses match the JG 2 claim of a Blenheim destroyed.)

At this point in time, the defence of the Western Front by the Luftwaffe was left to just these two Jagdgeschwaders. JG 2 defended the airspace to the south of the Seine, and JG 26 to the north and up to Holland. In many ways, this makes any detailed analysis of the day's events very much simpler, with only the reports of JG 26 to consider in respect of Circus 68. However, the battle which ensued is still complex and confusing when it comes to trying to make some sense of what really happened between the two opposing sides.

The pilot to whom Galland referred in his interview with the author was Leutnant Wolfgang Kosse, the Staffelkapitän of 5/JG 26 – although if we are to take at face value the German reports on his victory then it would most certainly rule him out as the pilot who downed Bader. The official list of statistics that gives Luftwaffe shoot downs states that the Kosse "kill" was timed at 11.40. If this is accurate, and it probably is, then it is much later than the time we know Bader to have been lost, i.e. around 11.20 when he called "Stay with me" as he went into action. Indeed, another report (the actual II/JG 26 victory list) times it even later at 11.45. It is fair to assume, therefore, that Kosse got his claim somewhere between 11.40 and 11.45. Not only that, but, significantly, the claim can also be ruled out on another factor. Kosse's attack was recorded to have taken place at 3,000m (10,000ft) which was considerably lower than the 24,000ft at which we know Bader was attacked. So, Leutnant Kosse cannot have been the victor although it has frequently, and quite wrongly, been assumed that Kosse was the pilot to whom Bader was introduced. Not only was he not the man who shot down Bader but he was certainly not the pilot randomly selected to play the role of victor for the benefit of the captured RAF wing leader, either!

Clearly, from what is known of Galland's account in *The First and the Last*, he did not consider himself as a contender for Bader's "kill". Indeed, he confirmed this during the 1977 interview when he went on to say; "I'd have liked his scalp myself!" Not only that, but the timing, altitude and location of Galland's claim cannot be made to fit at all. The report of his combat is very specific:

At 11.32 Galland attacked a Spitfire at 4,000m (13,000ft) north-west of St Pol. He attacked the 'plane from behind and below using one MG 151 and two cowl-mounted MG 131s at a distance of 100 to 20m. The 'plane burst into flames with dark plumes of smoke. Parts of the 'plane came off, such as plates from around the fuselage. The 'plane dived into the water and the pilot baled out and landed close to [Cumole?]

Apart from the time and altitude discrepancy the most telling feature of this report that rules out Bader is a crash into the sea. We know for certain that Bader's crash was inland, and many miles from the French coast. Whoever Galland got, it certainly wasn't Bader, and in fact it defies all attempts at identification. When we look at all the RAF losses in that action, none fit at all – nor are the facts of those losses anywhere close to what Galland reported. It is possible that he attacked and then followed down a British fighter towards the sea, but the splash he saw was perhaps a fountain of water thrown up by one of the bombs being dropped by the exiting Blenheims. It was certainly not a crashing fighter.

Flying with Galland in the Geschwader Stab that day was Oberleutnant Johannes Schmid, and he too filed a combat report claiming a downed Spitfire. Schmid was flying a Messerschmitt 109 F4 and was with Galland when he shot at another Spitfire. As he was pulling away he saw a Spitfire flying alone which he attacked twice at 2,500m (8,202ft) from behind and opened fire at a distance of between 80 – 50m. He shot the aircraft down using a total of sixty cannon rounds and 240 machine-gun rounds approximately 10km to the east of St Omer, watching flames and dark plumes of smoke coming off the aircraft as the pilot baled out at around 11.25.

Unteroffizier Richter, who was flying with him, witnessed the pilot's parachute opening and saw the Spitfire go down to the north of St Omer on the edge of a forest. He clearly saw the crash as he flew down to 300m (1,000ft). Again, we have an altitude discrepancy which would rule out Bader being Schmid's victim. In any case, we can easily tie up a pretty definite contender for the British pilot who fell to Schmid's hail of cannon and machine-gun fire. Interestingly, though, we can be absolutely certain that Schmid was the pilot introduced to Bader as his victor. On 21 August 1941 he was awarded the Knight's Cross after twenty-five aerial victories. The German Propaganda Kompanie, writing on 24 August of Schmid's decoration, told how; "....a few days before, Schmid had forced an opponent to bale out after trying to attack one of his comrades. The meeting of these two men, the German and the wing commander, in the headquarters of the Geschwader was an exceptional experience. The Englishman went to his victor, laid a hand on his shoulder and said with clear respect in his voice, 'I have mastered the art of flying in my career and I can fly! But you can do it better!'" It seems, therefore, that Galland's arbitrary nomination as a victor had stuck with Schmid – at least so far as the German propaganda machine was concerned.

This is Spitfire P8361 "Krakatoa" which carried Sgt G B "Barry" Haydon to his death on Circus 68, falling to the guns of Oblt Schmid. Here, it is pictured during its earlier service with 303 Squadron. *(via W Matusiak)*

Unfortunately, none of the evidence backs up this pilot as the actual victor. Schmid was certainly introduced as Bader's nemesis, but in fact he had shot down Sergeant G B Haydon, RAAF.

Sergeant Haydon was flying Spitfire IIA P8361 (a presentation aeroplane named "Krakatoa") with 452 Squadron in the Kenley Wing when he was lost on Circus 68. The circumstantial report of his commanding officer stated:

> Whilst operating with Circus 68 over France on 9/8/41 at about 11.20 hours Sergeant Haydon was Green two. Green one was Pilot Officer Truscott who reports that during an engagement with a number of Me 109s at about 10,000ft he suddenly missed Sergeant Haydon who had disappeared from his view.

Clearly, the time and altitude match quite closely to Schmid's report and we can also place the crash location on the ground, too, which adds to the certainty of confirmation. Post-war, the Missing Research & Enquiry Unit of the RAF searched for the 40,000 plus RAF casualties lost in north-west Europe between 1939-45 and whose graves had not yet been located. In the case of Haydon, the scene of the crash at Forêt de Tournehem was investigated by the MREU who found that Haydon had baled out too low and died from his injuries after landing in a tree, despite the ministrations of a local doctor, Dr Lamirault. Carved onto that tree by French woodcutters and still visible to the MREU team in 1947 was the wording, "Il mort pour la France 1941". Sergeant Gerald Haydon lies buried not far away in the cemetery at Longuenesse, St Omer. There is really no doubting that Schmid was responsible for shooting down Haydon given the near perfect match of detail. Haydon's Spitfire crash location at the Forêt de Tournehem on 9 August 1941 would also usefully be ruled out later in the author's investigation as a possible contender for Bader's crash site.

Ten minutes after the Schmid victory that Richter was able to confirm and geographically "fix" for the JG 26 intelligence officer, Richter himself claimed another Spitfire. This one, like Galland's claim, he also reported as having fallen into the sea north of Dunkirk. Again, and like Galland's claim, it simply cannot be substantiated against any of the RAF losses in that action.

Oberfeldwebel Walter Meyer of 6/JG 26 is the next claimant in the interception of Circus 68 to scrutinise, although information on his "kill" is scant. All that we have recorded is that he shot down a Spitfire between 11.25 and 11.35 in the St Omer region. Nothing more. Certainly, the timing and location fits broadly with Bader but it seems unlikely that Meyer's claim would not have been closely scrutinised by JG 26 staff officers to see if his "kill" was indeed Bader. By Galland's testimony we know that the victorious pilot could not be identified – officially at least! In previously published works Meyer has been quoted as a "likely" or "possible" victor for Bader, but in reality there exists absolutely nothing tangible on which to base this premise. In fact, there are two more Spitfire losses on Circus 68 who one might argue could just as equally fit the bill; Pilot Officer O'Byrne and Sergeant Chapman, both of 452 Squadron.

The only other remaining contenders to have possibly taken out the RAF's legless hero are Oberfeldwebel Erwin Busch and Oberleutnant Erwin Biederman, both of them pilots of 9/JG 26. Busch made a claim at the right time, but in an unknown location, and the circumstances of the shoot down are also unknown. As for Biederman, an ex-Fiesler test pilot who had recently joined JG 26, his claim was made at an unknown time and location and could therefore be during the unrelated combat in which JG 26 was involved in the late afternoon of that same day. Again, it is hard to imagine that if Busch or Biederman had been involved with the famous Tangmere wing leader then their claims would not have been scrutinised and linked.

Only one more JG 26 claim for that day is left on the table. However, it will be seen later in this chapter that the circumstances of that particular victory are so clearly recorded and identifiable as to rule out completely any link to Bader. Before we examine the detail of this combat claim, however, it is necessary to look at what Douglas Bader claimed had brought him down; collision.

There can be no doubt that the sledgehammer blows which disabled Bader's aeroplane were sudden, catastrophic to the airframe and utterly overwhelming to the senses of the pilot. If it was the case that Bader's tail and rear fuselage were hit repeatedly by a burst, or bursts, of cannon shells then the disastrous effects of such an onslaught might well have appeared to be the result of a collision. If, as we will suggest here, Bader was hit by cannon fire he could probably have been excused for genuinely believing that something had collided with him from behind. The instantaneous loss of elevator and rudder control and the pitching forward of the aeroplane registered in Bader's brain to be indicative of the loss of his tail – and collision seemed to explain it.

In fact, if one considers the possibility of a concentration of 20mm explosive cannon shells slamming into the rear end of a Spitfire in a second or so, and also take into account that the explosive content of just a single shell was considered to be roughly equivalent to that of a hand grenade, then it is very easy to visualise the destructive power of such a salvo. Blowing away the tail unit or rear fuselage – or large parts thereof – could well be an inevitable consequence of such hits. Certainly, though, we cannot find a victor to match his loss through gunfire. Surely, then, we have to accept the collision version of events. Or do we?

The first difficulty one would imagine we might have is in identifying a likely contender for a collision given that so many Messerschmitt 109s were blasted out of the sky and lost during Circus 68. How are we going to know which Messerschmitt it was? Yet, when looking at the Luftwaffe loss and damage lists for the day, that difficulty is justifiably replaced by some puzzlement as the task becomes apparently easy. There are, in fact, only two contenders for the collision: Firstly, Unteroffizier Albert Schlager of 3/JG 26 whose crash was near Aire-sur-la-Lys, in the right place, right in the combat zone, and at the right time. However, II/JG 26 lost another Me 109 that day, its unnamed pilot baling out at Merville some twenty kilometres to the east of the combat zone. We do not know the time of that incident (it could have therefore been during the late afternoon action, or perhaps unrelated to either action) and the German quartermaster returns for the Luftwaffe show it just as a "crash" and do not specifically relate it to combat. So, Schlager must therefore be our collision victim. Who then were the other fourteen Me 109s shot down that day – given that no other Luftwaffe fighter units were engaged?

For now, assuming someone did collide with Bader, then let us just place Schlager in the frame as the only pilot who could possibly have flown into the Tangmere wing leader's Spitfire. After all, there are not any damaged aeroplanes referenced in the meticulously accurate listings made on a daily basis by the Luftwaffe quartermaster general that could in any way fit.

These listings, it is important to note, were not made with a view to "massaging" loss figures or with any form of propaganda in mind. Instead, they were produced as a daily stock-take in order to ensure replenishment of losses and maintenance of all units at full or adequate strength and were for internal use only. Both one hundred percent losses and damaged machines were recorded here. At the very least, in the unlikely event that a fighter had collided in mid-air and its pilot survived to nurse back a damaged 'plane then one would expect to find a filed report of perhaps a thirty, fifty or seventy percent damaged machine. No such reports were filed for 9 August 1941. Not for any degree of damage. Not only that, but one would have expected a report from the pilot to have been made for such an extraordinary event as a mid-air collision with one of the RAF's "oberkannone", and certainly for Galland to have known about it – which he didn't.

Luftwaffe "ace" and Circus 68 combatant, Oblt Gerhard Schoepfel, who claimed Buck Casson as his thirty-third victory on 9 August 1941. *(courtesy S Hill)*

Hauptmann Gerhard Schoepfel, commander of III Gruppe JG 26, on the other hand was able to give an accurate and verifiable account of his claim over a Spitfire which was timed at approximately 11.45. It is an account we can clearly and very definitely attribute to a particular RAF pilot.

After the air battle and after my gruppe had split up, with the British on their homeward flight, I headed alone for my airfield at Liegescourt, near Crécy. Suddenly I saw a flight of four Spitfires flying westwards. I attacked them from above and after a short burst of fire the rear machine nosed over sharply and dived away. While the other aircraft flew on unconcerned I dived after the fleeing Spitfire as I could see no sign of damage. The British pilot hugged the ground, dodging shrubs, trees, and houses. I was constantly in his prop wash and could not aim properly. Because of the warm air near the ground my radiator flaps opened and my speed dropped off. It thus took a long time to obtain a good firing position.

Finally I was positioned immediately behind the Spitfire and it filled my gun sight. I pressed the firing knob for my cannon and machine guns, and…click. I had apparently exhausted my ammunition in the earlier air battles. Under no circumstances did I want to give up the chase. The British pilot had no way to know my condition and I wanted to strike terror in him for as long as he was over French soil. I thus stayed right behind him, at high speed.

Suddenly, to my utter disbelief, I saw a white plume of smoke behind the Spitfire. The smoke grew more dense; the propeller soon came to a stop and the pilot made a crash landing in a field east of Marquise. I circled the aircraft, noted its markings (for the victory report), saw the pilot climb out, and waved at him. Just as German soldiers approached him he was able to ignite a built-in explosive charge which destroyed the centre section of the aircraft. I returned to my airfield and sent my ordnance officer to the site to determine the reason for the forced landing.

The pilot was a British flight lieutenant. The ordnance officer found, to my astonishment, that the aircraft had taken a single machine-gun round in an engine cylinder during my first attack. Had I not pressed after the pilot and forced him to fly at top speed he would probably have reached England despite the damage. Just a few weeks before, I myself had made it back over the Channel after two of my engine connecting rods had been smashed over Dover. The British pilot had to head for prison camp, while I recorded my thirty-third victory.

Schoepfel, who would succeed Galland as kommodore of JG 26 that December, may have visited the crash site of the Spitfire he had downed. Certainly, he had it photographed but this may have been by the ordnance officer or other members of JG 26. We know, of course, that it was not Bader's aeroplane. However, it is significant that Schoepfel either visited the wreck or had it photographed, and this begs the question; if any of the JG 26 pilots were the definite victor over Bader then, surely, they too would have done the same. It seems inconceivable that they wouldn't have, and had they done so then surely some sort of photographic evidence would have survived and surfaced by now? In the case of Schoepfel's victim, he was much less of a "prize" than the famous Bader. He was, though, it would turn out, a highly significant player in the battle of Circus 68 and Bader's demise that day. He was Flight Lieutenant Lionel Harwood Buck Casson, B Flight commander, 616 Squadron.

The wreck of Buck Casson's Spitfire at Les Attaques after he had made a forced landing and then set fire to his aircraft. The YQ fuselage codes of 616 Squadron can be clearly seen. *(via Caldwell)*

Chapter Six

The Experiences of Buck Casson

Lionel Harwood Casson was one of the stalwarts of 616 Squadron. The son of a Sheffield steel buyer he joined 616 as an auxiliary at Doncaster on 6 April 1939 and, after the outbreak of war, went to 2 Flying Training School at Brize Norton before rejoining the squadron at Leconfield on 6 April 1940. From here, he was then sent to 6 Operational Training Unit at Sutton Bridge on 28 April 1940 from where a posting to 501 Squadron, flying Hurricanes in France, followed on 15 May.

It was a brief sojourn, though. Before he could join the squadron his train was bombed outside Amiens and he lost all his kit in the attack. He succeeded in making his way through all the prevailing chaos and back to Cherbourg from where he escaped by sea back to England. Briefly posted to 79 Squadron, flying Hurricanes at Biggin Hill, he managed to work a transfer back to 616 Squadron at Leconfield on 7 July just in time for the Battle of Britain. As a fighter pilot, his success rate was certainly respectable even though he did not rise to "ace" status in the accepted sense. Nonetheless, his score sheet reads as follows:

15 August 1940 – $\frac{1}{2}$ Junkers 88
30 August 1940 – He 111 probable
30 August 1940 – He 111 probable
1 September 1940 – Bf 109 probable
1 September 1940 – Do 17
5 May 1941 – $\frac{1}{2}$ Ju 88
22 June 1941 – $\frac{1}{2}$ Bf 109
24 June 1941 – Bf 109 damaged
26 June 1941 – Bf 109
19 July 1941 – Bf 109 probable
23 July 1941 – Bf 109
23 July 1941 – Bf 109 damaged

So, as we can see, a respectable combat score reflecting Casson's ability as a fighter pilot. Certainly he was no rookie. Moreover, in addition to the tally shown above, and not shown in any previously listed score, we now know that Casson also claimed a Bf 109 destroyed on 9 August 1941 which is clearly significant in the context of this work.

Casson was to serve with 616 Squadron for the rest of his RAF career, and was released from the RAF in November 1954 as squadron leader, DFC, AFC, and, by then, officer commanding 616 Squadron. As a pilot, he was rated above average and certainly became

Spitfire P7753 "Pampero One" of 616 Squadron at RAF Tangmere during April 1941. This aircraft was flown by Flt Lt Buck Casson when he was shot down by a Junkers 88 on 5 May 1941, baling out near Littlehampton. At this time 616 Squadron aircraft were wearing QJ code letters, but had changed to YQ prior to Circus 68.

a good, solid, steady and reliable pilot on 616 Squadron – well liked and well respected by all ranks. An affable and friendly type who was chalk to Bader's cheese. In 1940, though, the two were yet to meet and would not do so until Bader joined the Tangmere Wing in the early spring of 1941.

On 5 May 1941 Casson suffered his first experience of being shot down whilst serving with the Tangmere Wing and, afterwards, faced the sharp and unforgiving tongue of his wing leader. On that day, during the morning, both Casson and Flying Officer Roy Marples were scrambled from Tangmere to intercept an unidentified plot at 15,000ft over Portsmouth. Climbing up through a thick blanket of haze, and approaching from the south-east, they located a lone aircraft some miles ahead which they were able to identify as a Junkers 88 when they gradually closed range. Before the pair were able to mount a surprise attack the German pilot spotted his pursuers and slammed his aeroplane into a full-throttle dive away to the south.

Steadily closing on the Ju 88 the pair finally caught up with it just fifty feet from the waves and now way out over the English Channel. Marples, out to starboard, had gained slightly on Casson in their initial diving turn and went in first to attack. Casson followed, firing a burst which silenced the troublesome rear guns of the Junkers but each time he closed for another attack he was out-manoeuvred by his quarry. A long way out to sea, and having lost sight of Marples, Casson suddenly realised that he had a steadily rising engine temperature.

A lucky (or unlucky) shot from the return fire had found its mark in his Spitfire's coolant system. Turning for home, he found the engine running roughly and he was also losing height. Worse, there were now glycol fumes in the cockpit. The danger of fire loomed and a bale out seemed inevitable. Deciding to hang on as long as he could, the haze suddenly cleared and he found himself over the coast near Littlehampton and began to head for nearby RAF Ford. He was at 1,200ft and decided to wait until he was down to 1,000ft before choosing whether to bale out or not. At that altitude he knew he would be cutting it a bit fine.

At 900ft, and still some minutes from Ford, the aeroplane was suddenly well alight and he realised it would be completely on fire by the time he landed. He had no desire to die in a blazing Spitfire. It was now or never. Jumping from the inferno and pulling his D-ring almost immediately the parachute cracked open, he swung once…and was down. He had landed behind a group of council houses at Poling, and his Spitfire plunged into woodland close to an army encampment at nearby Priors Leas Lane. It had been a close shave all round. But now he had to face Bader.

Back at Tangmere, the wing leader was furious. He thought a "sitter" had been let off the hook. Worse, one of his pilots had been so bloody silly and careless as to be shot down by a rear gunner – losing a perfectly good Spitfire into the bargain. He raged and fumed and "harrumphed" about the whole episode, expressing the view that he'd have never let it get away and would certainly never have allowed himself to be shot down by anyone – least of all by a rear gunner in a bloody bomber! He even glibly remarked that if the enemy was so heavily armoured from behind that they couldn't shoot it down then they should have shot underneath at the sea, allowing their bullets to ricochet up into the bomber's unprotected belly. Of course, it was a tongue-in-cheek remark but Bader was making the point that although the pair might have missed the Junkers they couldn't possibly have missed the sea! These were comments that were perhaps indicative of the man and not least his sense of personal invincibility; that he was simply too good a shot to miss an easy target, or too good to be shot down himself. Nobody would ever get him.

In fact, the Junkers 88 attacked by Casson and Marples on 5 May 1941 managed to limp back to France. The aircraft, peppered by over fifty hits, was flown by Leutnant Heinrich Brinkmann of 5/Aufkl Gr 122 who succeeded in getting his damaged Junkers 88, F6 + CN, down at Haute Fontaine following the rude interruption of his early morning reconnaissance mission to Bournemouth, Southampton and Portsmouth.

As we know, Casson did not come back from Circus 68. Like Bader, he was now a prisoner of war. Initially, the two spent some time together at the same camp but later on Bader was moved to Colditz Castle. It was from here that he was released on 14 April 1945 and we know that one of the first things he did upon his return to the UK was to write to Casson. We do not, unfortunately, have the transcript of Bader's letter to Casson, but we do have Casson's reply dated 28 May 1945. From the date of that letter it would seem that Bader was apparently in some haste to get hold of Casson's version of events relating to 9 August 1941.

When the author first contacted Casson during the early 1970s it was, initially, to discuss the episode of his bale out on 5 May 1941. Later, in another long discussion, Casson ventured to offer that he had had "some involvement" the day Bader was lost. At first, and during conversations in the early 1980s, his comments were a little ambiguous but led the author to discuss, privately, with others the possibility that it had been Casson who had collided with Bader. This, of course, was before the author's knowledge of the full facts and, at this stage, none of the detailed research that forms the basis of this book had been embarked upon. However, it was not long before the nature of Casson's demise was unearthed (i.e. a shoot down by Schoepfel) and his "involvement" with Bader's loss seemed simply to be that both of them had been unfortunate enough to have been brought down and taken PoW on the same day. Nothing more.

All the same, Buck was not over keen to discuss the issue with the author (not always unusual when it comes to combatants discussing capture and imprisonment) but he promised to produce something which would be of interest. Finally, some while later, on 12 February 1990, he did so. Enclosed with his letter was a copy of the one he had written to Bader on 28 May 1945. Its preamble was just the usual chatty stuff one might expect about personal plans and prospects for the future, family life etc. What Bader wanted, though, was the whole story through Casson's eyes. And he certainly got it:

Now for the day we disgraced the Tangmere Wing and you say you want the whole story – phew.

When we dived to attack those Me 109s that were climbing up in formation I was to starboard and behind you with three other aircraft of B Flight. My number two was a Rhodesian sergeant whose name I have forgotten and Roy Marples was on my right with his number two.

I watched you attack with A Flight and break to port as I was coming in. I was well throttled back in the dive as the other three started to fall behind and I wished to keep the flight together. I attacked from the rear and, after having a squirt at two 109s flying together, I left them for a single one flying inland alone. I finished nearly all my cannon up on this boy who finally baled out at about 6,000ft having lost most of his tail unit. The other three B Flight machines were somewhere in my rear and probably one of the lads saw this.

Now I believe we had crossed at Hardelot some minutes in advance of the other squadrons from Tangmere for we were alone when we sighted and attacked the goons but by the time I had finished my little scrap the wing squadrons had joined and were all well above me and on their way out towards Hardelot again.

I climbed to about 13,000ft and fell in with Billy Burton and three other aircraft, all I believe from A Flight. We chased around in a circle for some time, gaining height all the while and the 109s were directly above us. Eventually we set off abreast and set off after the wing.

Billy had the other three A Flight machines with him flying in pairs abreast but about 200 yards out to starboard. We were repeatedly attacked by two Me 109s which followed us out and were flying behind and above us. Each time they started to dive I called out and we all turned and re-formed, the 109s giving up the attack and climbing again each time.

About fifteen miles inland from the coastline I saw another Spitfire well below us and about half a mile to starboard. This machine was alone and travelling very slowly. I assumed the pilot to be in some trouble. I called up Billy and suggested that we cross over to surround him and help him back as he was such a sitter. I broke off to starboard and made for the solitary Spit and then, upon looking back for Billy and the other three, I was amazed to see them diving away to the south west for a low layer of cloud through which they soon disappeared. I realised then that my message had either been misunderstood or had never been received.

Like a greenhorn I had been watching Billy's extraordinary disappearance to the left and the lone Spitfire below to my right and had lost sight of the two 109s that had been worrying us. I remember looking for them but upon not discovering their position I had assumed that they had chased Billy. I was soon proved wrong however when I received three hits somewhere in the fuselage and wing. This occurred just as I was coming alongside the lone Spitfire which I couldn't identify as it was not from Tangmere. I broke for some cloud at 5,000ft which I found too thin for cover and was followed by the two 109s.

I now picked out two more 109s flying above me so decided to drop to zero feet, fly up north and cross the Channel at a narrow point as I was not sure of the damage I had received and the engine was definitely not going normally. I pressed the teat and tried to run for it but the two 109s behind had more speed and were rapidly within range, whilst the other two flew 1500ft above and dived from port to starboard and back putting in quick bursts. Needless to say, I was not flying straight and level all this time.

In the event, I received a good one from behind which passed between the stick and my right leg and took some of the rudder bar off on its way. It passed into the petrol tank and whether it went on into the engine I don't know. Petrol began to leak into the cockpit, oil pressure was dropping low and with the radiator wide open I could smell the glycol heating.

As the next attack came I pulled straight up from the deck in a loop and on my way down, as I was changing direction towards the sea, my engine became extremely rough and seized up and the white glycol fumes poured forth. There was nothing to do but crash land the aircraft.

I tried to send you a hurried message as I had no idea you were also in trouble. I then blew up the wireless and made a belly landing in a field about ten miles south of Calais. The goons, upon seeing the glycol, were decent enough not to shoot me up as I was landing but circled about for a time and gave my position away to a German cavalry unit in a wood at a corner of the field.

Setting fire to the aircraft was an easy matter as I was carrying a "Portfire" and the cockpit was full of petrol but I had no sooner done this than a party of shrieking goons with rifles came chasing over and that was the end of me. What eventually happened to the lone Spit I went to help out I have no idea but as the 109s followed me he must have been OK. I hope so.

Well DB, that is the story and one I shall never forget I suppose, for I have gone over that bloody day so often in my daydreams.

Here we have a very clear and concise account of what happened that day from the perspective of Flight Lieutenant Buck Casson himself. It is a fascinating tale to read, and written when it was relatively fresh in his mind it can surely be regarded as reliable. In almost every respect it matches the account of Schoepfel and we can therefore be absolutely sure that it was he who shot Casson down. Writing to the author in 1990, Buck Casson filled in some detail of the aftermath of his shoot down:

It just so happened that the German unit who captured me were being visited or inspected by a German general in all his regalia. Brought before him I made an effort to show some respect for his rank but having no knowledge of the language I have no idea what he said to me. We were on the outskirts of St Omer (sic) and I was marched a short distance to a Luftwaffe office beside the main road where I was searched and my possessions were confiscated – later to be returned to me except for one identity disc. After some time a Luftwaffe engineer officer arrived from Gravelines to tell me my "friend" Bader was in hospital there. I could hardly believe it. When questioned I would only admit to having heard of him in the service.

Casson, like Bader, was "in the bag". But what of the Messerschmitt 109 he claimed that day?

Setting aside all of the other RAF Fighter Command claims on Circus 68 for the moment, and looking only at Casson's, we need to take at face value his account, i.e. using up all his cannon ammunition, shooting the tail off a Messerschmitt 109 and watching as its pilot finally baled out at about 6,000ft. As we have seen, there can really be only one contender for all of the RAF claims in that action. Unteroffizier Albert Schlager who was shot down and killed near St Omer. But was he Casson's victim?

12th February 1990

...aunders,

for your letter of the 6th February and for the
...ng brochure. As you say, it is quite a long time
...were in touch and I hope you are still in good

...ng the 9th August 1941 episode, I am enclosing a
...a letter I wrote to Douglas Bader after our release
...arceration in 1945; as you may know we were the only
...n the Tangmere Wing to be shot down that day.

...the letter to Douglas covers only part of the story
...try to add further details as I can recollect them.

...ag comprised 616 and 610 Squadrons based at Westhampnet
...5 Squadron at Merston. Douglas most always flew with
...a the time we engaged the other
...d we took off on an offensive sortie ahead of the other
...ons which had not caught up by the time to have ample height
...rons and it was quite a novel experience to be underdog.......
...n attack instead of being in the role of underdog......
......

...ally came to rest in a field on one side of which was a
...e wherein there was a troop of German soldiers and it
...so happened that they were being visited or inspected
...n Army General in all his regalia. Brought before him
...ade an effort to show some respect for his rank but
...ng no knowledge of the language I have no idea what
...said to me. We were on the outskirts of St. Omer and
...as marched a short distance to a Luftwaffe office beside
...main road where I was searched and my possessions were
...afiscated, later to be returned to me except for one
...entity disc. After some time a Luftwaffe engineer officer
...rived from Gravlines to tell me my "friend" Bader was in
...spital there. I could hardly believe it and when
...estioned I would only admit to having heard of him in
...e Service.

...was then taken to a room above the office and overlooking
...he main road; a French window opened onto a small balcony
...and because this offered a means of escape two guards
...remained with me that night. Early next morning, accompanied
...by two different guards, I was taken by car to the railway
...station and by train via Liege and Cologne to Frankfurt en
...Main. Here my guards handed me over to another pair and
...we drove to Stalag Luft at Oberusel. By that time I was
...feeling more than a little miserable having had no sleep,
...nothing to eat and only a quick rinse in cold water. Upon
...arrival I was stripped of all but my underclothing and
...placed in solitary confinement for 1½ days, during which
...time I was interrogated and presented with dubious looking
...questionnaires to fill in. Eventually when it was realised
...I was not prepared to do more than give my name, rank and
...number, my clothes were returned and I was ushered into the
...P.O.W. compound where I remained for about ten days before

---

- 2 -

being sent with others to Oflag X C outside Lubeck. This
was something of a straff or reprisal camp for Crete
survivors and held about 750 prisoners, most of whom were
army men. Conditions were extremely poor and it was a
great relief after about two months, following a visit
by representatives of the then American Protecting Power,
to learn that the camp was to be evacuated. Shortly
thereafter we were transported to Oflag VI B at Dossel
Warburg north west of Kassel to be joined by Ps.O.W.
from other camps during the next few days. There I met
up with four army friends from home who had been captured
at St. Valery and in Greece, several RAF chums and Douglas
Bader for the first time since our take off from Westhampnet...
....

I hope you can piece together the sad train of events from
this rather long-winded letter and the copy of that I sent
to Bader. All I would add is the number W3458 of the
Spitfire V B I was flying on the 9th August 1941 but
regret I do not have a photograph of the aircraft.

Also as a matter of interest I am enclosing a copy of an
extract from the Luftwaffe JG26 Diary from which it seems
clear that Adolf Galland was the pilot who clobbered me.
This information was obtained for me from the Public
Records Office, Kew Gardens, by a very helpful and
interested local newspaper reporter in 1977.

I'm afraid time passes all too quickly, but I still
have hopes of visiting the Tangmere museum and seeing
how the whole area must have altered over the years.

Best wishes,

Yours sincerely,

"Buck" Casson.

The letter sent by Buck Casson to Bader and supplied by Casson to the author.

- 2 -

...ly had the other three A flight machines with him flying in pairs
...east and I flew abreast but about 200 yards starboard. We were
...ndly attacked by two ME 109's which followed us out and were
...' and above us. Each time they started to dive I called
...' and reformed - the 109's giving up the attack

...line I saw another Spit well below
...This machine was alone and travelling
...to be in some trouble. I called up Billy
...surround him and made for the solitary
...to starboard and the other three, I was
...or Billy and the other three, I was
...rd to the south west for a low layer of
...appeared. I realised then that my message
...had never been received.

...ching Billy's extraordinary disappearance
...below to my right and had lost sight of the
...ng us. I remember looking for them but
...ition I had assumed that they had chased
...ng however when I received three hits some-
...8. This occurred just as I was coming along-
...couldn't identify as it was not from Tangmere.
...00 ft which I found too thin for cover and was

...109's flying above me so decided to drop to zero
...oss the Channel at a narrow point as I was not
...received and the engine was definitely not going
...teat and tried to run for it but the two 109's
...d were rapidly within range, whilst the other two
...d dived from port to starboard and back putting in
..., to say, I was not flying straight and level all

...ved a good one from behind which passed between the
...e and took some of the rudder bar off on its way.
...etrol tank and whether it went on into the engine
...pit was full of petrol but I had no sooner done this than a
...Petrol began to leak into the cockpit, oil pressure
...i with the radiator wide open I could smell the glycol

...came I pulled straight up from the deck in a loop and
..., I was changing direction towards the sea, my engine
...rough and seized up and the white glycol fumes poured
...nothing to do but crash land the aircraft.

...you a hurried message as I had no idea you were also in
...a blew up the wireless and made a belly landing in a field
...south of Calais. The goons, upon seeing the glycol, were
...not to shoot me up as I was landing but they circled about for
...e my position away to a German cavalry unit in a wood at a
...field.

...to the aircraft was an easy matter as I was carrying a portfire
...pit was full of petrol but I had no sooner done this than was the
...rieking goons with rifles came chasing over and that was the

---

28th May 1945

Dear Douglas,

Many thanks for your letter and I hope you are as full of vigour as
you were when I last saw you at VIB.

I read of your safe arrival in England when I was still near Lubeck
and wondered how you would enjoy being an aerial passenger after all
this time.

Your letter is full of questions so I will attempt to answer them in
order.

Firstly, I am well and very fit but I have no plans as yet. I heard
a rumour at Rheine that all auxiliary squadrons were being recalled
to England for re-grouping etc. and that it was likely they would
remain in England for some sort of home defence. I think it sounds
rather attractive but how true the story is I cannot say. I hate the
thought of leaving the RAF and intend to hang on as long as possible.
A P.C. of course would be the ideal thing, but age and experience are
against me due to these last four lousy years and I am sure I could
never pass the examinations. Another "fly in the ointment" is that
I am not over enthusiastic about the Far East, partly because I have
lost contact with the old gang, but mainly due to conditions here at
home which are not too rosy. What I wish to avoid at all costs is
a lengthy stay on the ground at some place like Cosford. What I
want to do is to have some more flying (not heavies) i.e. ferrying
to Middle East, policing West Germany, Home Defence.

Now for the day we disgraced the Tangmere Wing and you say you want
to whole story - phew.

When we dived to attack those ME 109's that were climbing up in formation
I was to starboard and behind you with three other aircraft of B flight.
My No. 2 was a Rhodesian sargeant whose name I have forgotten and Roy
Marples was on my right with his No. 2.

I watched you attack with A flight and break to port as I was coming in.
I was well throttled back in the dive as the other three started to fall
behind and I wished to keep the flight together. I hate the
and, after having a squirt at two 109's flying together, I attacked from the rear
a single one flying inland alone. I finished nearly all my canon up on
this boy, who finally bailed out at about 6,000 feet, having lost most of
his tail unit. The other three 'B' flight machines were somewhere in my
rear and probably one of the lads saw this.

Now I believe we had crossed at Hardlot some minutes
squadrons from Tangmere for us were ......
...goons but he...

CHAPTER SEVEN

THE LOSS OF UNTEROFFIZIER SCHLAGER

During the author's initial field investigations of the Bader story in the St Omer area in 2004, the landing site of Douglas Bader by parachute was located just to the north-east of Boeseghem. Not only that, but the crash site of what was believed to be a Messerschmitt 109 was pointed out by local researcher and historian, Georges Goblet. Georges had established that, according to local knowledge and information based on eyewitness accounts, the Messerschmitt had crashed just a minute or so before Bader landed by parachute. The German pilot, it was said, had baled out but fallen to his death when his parachute failed to deploy. If this account was accurate then it was certainly very interesting in the picture of the day's events. As reported, then, the facts of this pilot's death fitted all the known circumstances appertaining to Schlager, but these local reports were only hearsay. Nothing more. Indeed, as we shall see, some local information relating to the supposed Bader crash site had already proved unreliable. In the case of the supposed Me 109 crash site, no hard documentary or physical evidence existed to link it with Circus 68. Some had to be found.

The German aeroplane in question had seemingly crashed into a marshy meadow behind 150 Route d'Hazebrouck, just to the north of Aire-sur-La-Lys (not through the roof of a farmhouse as suggested by another author), and buried itself deeply in the soft soil upon impact. Using Georges Goblet's information, the crash was easily located and on 15 June 2004 the author organised an excavation of the site. Utilising a mechanical excavator the site was investigated down to a depth of some thirty feet, although not without some considerable difficulty. Just before thirty feet, and as the excavation began to get very unstable and with all the substantial wreckage clearly getting beyond reach, a number of artefacts were retrieved – these being primarily from the tail and rear fuselage section. Amongst them were pieces of yellow fabric from the rudder, parts of both horizontal stabilisers, sections of both elevators, portions of fin bearing traces of the swastika and the complete tail oleo leg and wheel. There were portions, too, of torn off engine cowling, also painted yellow, and broken pieces of engine ancillary equipment which had been smashed away on impact.

Very clearly, this was an aeroplane that had gone into the ground with its tail section substantially intact. But which one? And was it associated with the battle of Circus 68? Careful cleaning of the recovered wreckage yielded a vital clue – a small alloy tag indicating this to be an Erla-built machine and with the werke nummer 8350. At last, the first definite piece of the Bader jigsaw puzzle was in place. Messerschmitt 109 F, number 8350, was identified in Luftwaffe records to have been the machine flown by Unteroffizier Albert Schlager during the morning action of 9 August 1941. There was, after all, a Circus 68 connection with this crash.

The discovery, though, raised rather more questions than it answered. Firstly, Casson was quite definite about "his" Messerschmitt 109 losing most of its tail before the pilot baled out – but here we had a Messerschmitt 109 that had gone into the ground with its tail unit just about intact. Not only that, but it was almost certainly the only Me 109 down in that action. Interestingly, though, the crash location was a matter of just four hundred

The tail wheel leg from Albert Schlager's Messerschmitt 109 F that was recovered from the crash site of the aircraft at Widdebrouck by the author in 2004. Its discovery helped rule this aircraft out as that claimed by Buck Casson.

yards from the Canal de Neufossé. Johnnie Johnson, when he had roared down through the cloud base and then pulled out of his dive after attacking a Messerschmitt 109, had observed "…wreckage burning on the ground near a canal". What he had seen, in fact, was the funeral pyre of Schlager's Messerschmitt after "Nip" Heppell had sent it into the ground. So what had Casson shot down?

Already, the uncomfortable possibility of "friendly fire" had emerged in the author's initial research of who-shot-down-who through the combat reports of the action. Now, it looked even more likely. The similarities between Bader's account of his own demise and Casson's

This tiny data plate recovered by the author from the crash site identifies the wreck as an Erla-built machine with the werke nummer 8350, thus proving it to have been the aircraft flown by Schlager lost during the Circus 68 engagement.

version of events that day are striking and inescapable. Bader says that he lost much of his tail unit and finally managed to get clear from his stricken Spitfire just before he entered cloud. From available meteorological evidence we know this to have been at around 5,000ft. Casson saw the pilot of "his" Messerschmitt "finally bale out at about 6,000ft". The inference of the wording *finally bale out* would certainly suggest quite strongly that the pilot had a degree of difficulty in getting out. Now, though, we were faced with some incontrovertible evidence; a Messerschmitt that we could confirm *had* been lost in the Circus 68 action and which *hadn't* lost its tail. With no other contenders for Casson's "kill", what was to be made of the facts now emerging?

Unteroffizier Albert Schlager of 3/JG 26 was a relatively novice fighter pilot, but that was not necessarily a significant factor in his loss. We do know that Schlager was caught from above and behind when his section of the 3rd Staffel climbed up from Clairmarais, their base at St Omer, while Bader and 616 Squadron dived down in the attack. It is likely that Schlager's section just happened to be the last of JG 26 getting off the ground, although

The Messerschmitt 109 Fs of I Gruppe JG 26 lined up along the perimeter of St Omer-Clairmarais. It was from here that Albert Schlager took off on his last flight during the morning of 9 August 1941 and it was to the building in the background that Bader's artificial leg was taken after its delivery and Bader himself after his escape. The building also fits the description of the location to where Buck Casson was first taken upon his capture. Still standing in 2007 its use then was as a hunting lodge. *(via Caldwell)*

more than one of the RAF pilots who took part that day thought it was a deliberate trap and that these climbing Messerschmitts of 3/JG 26, much lower than the Tangmere Wing, were the bait. Pilot Officer Tony Gaze was flying with 610 Squadron that day. He recalled:

Near the target Douglas Bader made a big mistake. We in 610 Squadron had seen some Me 109s below which he couldn't see and he told us not to attack. By the time he saw them he'd wasted a good few minutes, conditions had changed and he was caught in a trap. A large number of 109s came down from above so I called "Break! For Christ's sake BREAK!" as I couldn't give callsigns. These aircraft would have normally been engaged by 41 Squadron at top cover, but they weren't there! We were outnumbered by the 109s and made an undignified retreat. The German controllers had pulled off a perfect bounce with bait aircraft and Bader was led into the trap. Some people said it was his greed for victories.

Trap or no trap, bait or no bait, Albert Schlager had been despatched by Nip Heppell and just as the British fighter pilot had lost sight of the falling body of the unfortunate German as it entered the cloud, so it was seen by twenty-eight-year-old Therese Dernocourt, still tumbling over and over, when it emerged from the base of the cloud. At first, Therese mistook the violent gyrations to be those of a falling propeller and then realised, as it neared the ground, what it actually was. The body fell onto a pile of straw in Emile Delhay's meadow near Widdebrouck, making an indentation in the ground where it impacted. Schlager's broken body was almost immediately taken away by the Germans.

Albert Schlager, born in the Austrian town of Bad Ischl on 9 June 1920, was the son of Dr Schlager and had joined the Luftwaffe on 14 April 1939. By 23 April 1940 he was at his first flying school, progressing through to 2 Erganzungstaffel (Training Squadron) of JG 26 by 2 July 1941, thus becoming one of the fighter pilots trained "in-house" who were referred to in the RAF Bomber Command Assessment document (chapter one) before his eventual operational posting to 3/JG 26 on 21 July 1941.

The ehrenbuch (honour book) of JG 26 reports that Schlager was lost on 9 August 1941 on only his second combat flight while climbing up to engage the enemy. As they were climbing, a squadron of Spitfires dived down from the left and above (616 Squadron) and Schlager

When Bader commanded 242 Squadron during the Battle of Britain he added artwork to his Hurricane showing Hitler being kicked up the backside by a flying boot marked "242". Bader transferred this marking to his Spitfire P9766 at Tangmere, shown here with Sgts West, Brewer and Mabbett and Plt Off Heppell on the extreme right. *(Jeff West)*

was shot down without any of his comrades seeing what happened due to the fierce engagement in which they then became embroiled. It was only on the return of the Staffel that he was missed; his wrecked aeroplane and body being subsequently found near Aire, close to Hazebrouck. (Laid to rest by his comrades in the heroes cemetery at Wizernes, his grave was subsequently moved to the German war cemetery at Bourdon, north-west of Amiens, where he now lies.)

Without a doubt, then, Albert Schlager had fallen to the guns of Nip Heppell. Johnson had seen the wreckage burning on the ground and had geographically "fixed" it. With the excavation in 2004 proving the tail section to have been intact when the Messerschmitt hit the ground, we have the evidence that this cannot have been the Me 109 Buck Casson had described. In any case, with no other Me 109s lost in this action the theory of friendly fire, previously raised by the initial analysis of Casson's 1945 letter to Bader, now began to have rather more substance to it.

CHAPTER EIGHT

RAF FIGHTER COMMAND CLAIMS FOR CIRCUS 68

No examination of events on 9 August 1941 would be fair or balanced without a closer look at the RAF Fighter Command claims during Circus 68. Already, we have looked at German claims for "kills" over British fighters during that action and seen an apparent discrepancy between the tally of claims made by the Germans and the actual RAF losses. We have also looked at Casson's contemporary account of events that day, and how things were perceived by Bader himself. A closer examination of the other relevant RAF claims, though, throws up a good number of surprises. Once again, as a starting point, it is interesting to go to Paul Brickhill's commentary in *Reach for the Sky*.

Brickhill describes Bader's post-capture visit to Galland's geschwader at Audembert and tells how the interpreter present told Bader that on the day that he had been brought down the Luftwaffe got twenty-six Spitfires for no loss. Brickhill goes on to state that this was such

A group of 71 "Eagle" Squadron pilots with one of their Hurricanes. Taken in March 1941 this photo nevertheless includes four of the Circus 68 participants. They are: Plt Off S A Mauriello (extreme left), Flt Lt A Mamedoff (6th from left), Plt Off E Q "Red" Tobin (7th from left) and Plt Off W H "Bill" Nichols (extreme right).

Pilots of 111 Squadron during the early summer of 1941. Second from left is Sqn Ldr John McLean, the squadron CO. Centre is Flt Lt Brotchie, one of the flight commanders. The other flight commander, Flt Lt Lionel Pilkington DFM, is at far right. He did not participate in Circus 68, but was shot down and killed over France during Circus 100 on 20 September 1941.

obvious nonsense that it buoyed Bader up by confirming for him the RAF's views on "extravagant German claims". In fact, the real proportion of Luftwaffe v. RAF losses/claims on Circus 68 were exactly opposite to the view expressed by Brickhill, and apparently shared by Bader. If the German claims were extravagant then those of RAF Fighter Command were no less so. On a claim-by-claim basis, then, let us examine the RAF cases for asserting victories over Luftwaffe fighters during that action.

Taking the North Weald Wing first, we have the detailed combat report of Pilot Officer W R "Bill" Dunn flying a Hurricane with A Flight, 71 "Eagle" Squadron. His report makes for a fascinating read, and Dunn certainly had a hair-raising experience when flying Circus 68:

I was flying as White one in close escort to the bombers. After we were about fifteen to twenty miles into France my engine started surging and then it stopped. I was left about a mile and a half behind the rest of the formation. I was gliding at about 120mph down towards the clouds at 4,500ft when I saw a Me 109 about 2,000ft above and coming after me. He tried to shoot me from a top position. I pulled my aeroplane's nose up and fired through his hood at one hundred yards range. I then did a half roll and followed him. I kept shooting at him during the dive up to three hundred yards range. My engine started again after the half roll. We went through the clouds and just as we came out a second Me 109 flying under the clouds flew between the first Me 109 and myself.

I shot a piece off his starboard wing. He had already been shot up by someone else because there was glycol and some black smoke coming out of it. I followed the first Me 109 down to about nine hundred feet and saw him crash. I then flew back to Gravelines at about eight hundred feet. I could only get 120mph out of the 'plane. I was shot at by ack-ack at Gravelines which I crossed at six hundred feet. I shot back at some of the ack-ack posts. I crossed the Channel at about two hundred feet and was joined by two Spitfires of 403 (Canadian) Squadron. They brought me to Manston where I landed and had my engine repaired. I then flew back to North Weald.

Although it is a riveting and extraordinary story, there are absolutely no German losses that fit Dunn's claims. Whilst he may well have shot at something he certainly shot nothing down, and if he saw something crash then this can only be explained by his witnessing the crash

Gp Capt Victor Beamish DSO & Bar, DFC, AFC.

of one of the two 485 Squadron losses, Sergeant Haydon or Sergeant Chapman. As for the two 403 Squadron pilots who escorted him to Manston, it is unfortunately not possible from the squadron operations record book to identify who they may have been.

The next claims, also from the North Weald Wing, were apparently for one Messerschmitt 109 probably destroyed and one damaged. Both of them were claimed by 111 Squadron according to the Fighter Command summary for Circus 68 filed under AIR 25/200 at the national archive. This information, however, is somewhat ambiguous as the squadron operations record book for Circus 68 on 9 August 1941 does not make mention of any such claims. In addition, no pilot's personal combat reports for such claims can be located in the national archives although the claim detailed in the following paragraph may well be the one referred to. The operations record book for 111 Squadron does make a claim for a Messerschmitt 109 F destroyed during the later operation over France that day at 17.55hrs when Flight Lieutenant Kellett claimed to have sent one into the ground near Calais. Either way, and if 111 Squadron per-se *did* actually make such claims for Circus 68, then they certainly cannot be substantiated.

Also flying with the wing, and attaching himself to 111 Squadron, North Weald station commander, Group Captain Victor Beamish, did claim some success against the Messerschmitts of JG 26. Again, his combat report fills in the detail:

> Whilst operating with the North Weald Wing on Circus 68 against the power station at Gosnay, we acted as close escort wing to six (*sic*) Blenheims. French coast was crossed at Mardyck and shortly afterwards an Me 109 F dived and pulled up on me from below. I saw tracers going by. I immediately went into a tight turn and got on the tail of the enemy aircraft giving him a two-second burst. He fell away at once emitting glycol and black smoke and went into cloud. I claim this enemy aircraft as damaged.
>
> When over the target area (Gosnay) a further Me 109 F went past me. I turned on him following him and giving him a good burst from above and almost dead astern. The enemy aircraft immediately turned over on its back and fell through the cloud emitting black smoke and glycol. This aircraft is claimed as probably destroyed.
> (Claims: one Me 109 probably destroyed. One Me 109 F damaged.)

Although the typed body of Beamish's general report indicated his claim to comprise one Me 109 probably destroyed and one damaged, this was later amended, in handwriting, within the report's preamble to two Me 109s claimed as probable. There is little doubt that

Beamish engaged and shot at the enemy. Unfortunately, his "probably destroyed" claims are over optimistic and there is no evidence, either, that the two Messerschmitts were even damaged although it seems certain that his claims were those referred to as being made by 111 Squadron.

The story is much the same with 403 Squadron, where Pilot Officer Anthony, flying as number two to the wing leader, Wing Commander Stapleton, also claimed a Messerschmitt 109 as probably destroyed.

Plt Off K H Anthony (right) of 403 Squadron claimed one Me 109 F as "probably destroyed" on Circus 68 in Spitfire W3573 KH-K whilst flying as number two to the Hornchurch wing leader, Wg Cdr Stapleton. Centre is Plt Off D H Waldon, another pilot with 403 Sqn. Waldon returned safely from Circus 68 but was lost during the second operation of the day when he was shot down over St Omer and killed. On the left is Plt Off F K Orme, killed in action on 28 August 1941 when he was shot down off the Hook of Holland in Blenheim V6436 of 21 Squadron. This photo was taken during their training in Canada.

I was Wingco two (Wing Commander Stapleton) 403 Squadron acting as lower escort cover in company with 603 Squadron (centre) and 611 Squadron (top cover) accompanying six (*sic*) Blenheims on a raid on Gosnay. As the bombers were crossing target four Me 109 Fs were seen diving upon them from above us from a north-westerly direction. The wing commander immediately turned on them. Turning with him I opened fire on the leader and held a three-and-a-half-second burst of cannon and machine-gun fire on him. Aware of other Huns above I immediately pulled away to the right not waiting to see if any damage was done. As I was pulling up an Me 109 shot across in front. Tightening my turn I sighted on him and allowing the approximate deflection for a quarter astern attack I opened fire at one hundred yards with cannon and machine gun.

After about three seconds all the cannon shells were used and I continued with machine gun, the attack developing in line-astern until the enemy aircraft rolled onto his back and spun inverted. I followed him for a short distance down but soon left as the bombers and fighters had turned northwards and home. At the time of my departure the aircraft had not recovered from the inverted spin and from the manner in which it entered and spun it seemed likely the pilot did not have control. The enemy aircraft is claimed as probable.

Given the set criteria for entering a claim of "probable" (see Appendix C) Pilot Officer Anthony was fully justified in entering this claim as he did. The reality, though, is that Anthony's quarry was neither hit nor damaged, and certainly did not crash out of control. Once again, an RAF pilot had been deceived by a Luftwaffe fighter pilot taking violent evasive action.

A line up of 452 Squadron at Kenley, early summer 1941. Included in the group are a number of Circus 68 participants. These are: Sgt Paul Makin (extreme left), Flt Lt Brendan Paddy Finucane (4th left), Plt Off Ray Thorold-Smith (8th left), Sqn Ldr Bob Bungey (9th left), Plt Off Keith Bluey Truscott (2nd right) and Sgt Dick Gazzard (extreme right).

602 Squadron, one of the elements of the Kenley Wing, also filed for one Messerschmitt 109 probably destroyed, and two damaged. Flight Lieutenant T D Williams DFC claimed the probable and Squadron Leader "Al" Deere DFC & Bar, claimed the two damaged. Williams saw his Messerschmitt fall away trailing black smoke after firing two three-second bursts of cannon and machine-gun fire. Deere shot at three 109s, the first going down into cloud after "a biggish piece flew off". The second he saw go into a dive trailing a banner of black smoke. The third he chased down to ground level, fired, but saw no result. In all of these cases it seems the pilots were misled by the German fighters' evasive manoeuvres. It was

452 Squadron in the same wing, though, who made the most claims with no less than five Messerschmitt 109s chalked up as destroyed. None of their claims can be validated.

Pilot Officer K W "Bluey" Truscott, flying as Green one, filed the first report:

After the squadron had been initially attacked I took evasive action and at 10,000 to 12,000ft I saw three Messerschmitt 109s 500ft above and behind me. I did a steep turn and temporarily lost sight of the 109s. When I looked ahead again the first 109 had apparently attacked and overshot and was about thirty yards in front of me. I took a five-second burst and observed a considerable part of his tail unit fly off. The 109 slumped forward and I noticed his elevators missing. He went down vertically. I followed to about 5,000ft and saw him disappear below me at a terrific speed into low cloud at 1,000ft. I then noticed that my number two (Sergeant Haydon) had disappeared on the engagement.

Being alone I went into low cloud and crossed the French coast at Boulogne. The cloud which had been at about 1,000ft cleared over the coast and being attacked by anti-aircraft and machine-gun fire I dived to about 100ft and machine-gunned the harbour. Anti-aircraft followed me several miles out to sea but it was a considerable distance behind. This aircraft I claim as destroyed because the elevators and part of the rudder were shot away, and at 1,000ft the 109 was definitely out of control and heading for the ground at a terrific speed.

Once again, we have a Messerschmitt 109 going down with large parts of the tail missing. A pretty definite claim on the face of it. And yet we have no Messerschmitt 109 lost that could possibly fit the bill. Truscott's is a carefully detailed report, and we need to examine that detail and look at what was going on around him in order to understand better what it was that he saw and what it was that he shot at. The findings uncannily and uncomfortably echo the Casson/Bader engagement.

Spitfire P7973, the 452 Squadron Spitfire flown by Bluey Truscott on Circus 68. Truscott was most likely involved in one of the friendly fire episodes of Circus 68 whilst flying this aircraft. *(P Arnold)*

From the combat report of Sergeant Makin (Black two) it is recorded that 452 Squadron were engaged by Spitfires, and the account he gives – including the details of Sergeant Chapman's loss – is again very detailed. From it, we know that he saw Chapman's Spitfire going down with the top half of his rudder and the port tail plane missing. Makin goes on:

> He broke away gently from the formation and I followed him. He was flying perfectly level during a steady turn to the left, but we were then attacked by six aircraft out of the sun that were later identified as Spitfires. In turning to intercept these aircraft I lost sight of Sergeant Chapman who was not seen again. I had noticed that he had his hood open, which was closed when we left Manston. Failing to find Sergeant Chapman I joined a section of Spitfires above me and we found the bombers who were just returning and came back with them as far as Manston. I landed at West Malling to refuel at 12.02 and then proceeded to Kenley, landing at 12.45.

A Messerschmitt 109 F of III/JG 26, Yellow 6, during the early part of 1941. If Heppell was correct when he described seeing a large number six on the fuselage of the Messerschmitt that he shot down then this photograph could well be of Schlager's aeroplane, werke nummer 8350.

It is hard to escape the conclusion that, in his steep turn, Bluey Truscott, having lost sight of the Messerschmitts, suddenly found himself behind Spitfires of his own squadron and, assuming these to be the Messerschmitts he had been trying to turn on to, he attacked one of them from just thirty yards astern – blasting the tail of the aeroplane with a five second hail of fire. Black one (Chapman) stood little chance from such point blank range and lost large sections of his tail and rudder and went down at once. It was all over, literally, in just seconds and Truscott saw what he believed to be "his Messerschmitt" going down with parts of the tail missing – exactly as Makin had described the demise of his colleague, Chapman.

In the confusion that followed, and with Spitfire mixing it with Spitfire, other pilots of the squadron filed reports that can only reflect a situation where Lewis, Thorold-Smith,

The sergeant pilots of A Flight, 616 Squadron, during the spring of 1941 at Woodfield House near Tangmere. Top: Sgt Brewer (RNZAF), middle left: Sgt Smith, middle right: Sgt "Jeff" West (RNZAF), standing: Sgt Mabbett.

Chisholm and Finucane were all party to a friendly fire debacle. Lewis (White two) put some shots into another aircraft with Sergeant Chisholm, claiming half a victory with him. Chisholm (Yellow two) reported that the pilot baled out and the aircraft went down in flames. Once more, it is impossible to link this to any Luftwaffe loss. Quite simply, there are none – but we only have to look at other Spitfire losses in that action to find one that does fit these circumstances. Pilot Officer O'Byrne was the only loss where the aircraft went down in flames and the pilot baled out.

Flight Lieutenant Finucane, Red one, also seems to have joined this Spitfire-on-Spitfire fray. With Pilot Officer Thorold-Smith (Yellow one) the two of them shot at an aeroplane whose fuselage and tail plane "blew-up". (NB: there is no reason why a tail plane of an aircraft under attack should just "blow-up" and this terminology is more than likely a rather exuberant way of describing the disintegration of a tail section under cannon fire.)

Once dispatched, Finucane joined up with Chisholm and took part in the destruction of the "enemy aircraft" that went down in flames with its pilot baling out. It seems, then, that Truscott, Finucane and Thorold-Smith all shot at the same aircraft which is very likely to have been Sergeant Chapman's Spitfire, followed moments afterwards by an attack on O'Byrne's Spitfire. In fact, there can be no other explanation and it is the view of the author that this, after the incident involving Bader, was the second friendly fire episode of Circus 68. As for O'Byrne, it is quite likely that he was downed by Chisholm and Finucane, thus becoming friendly fire victim number three. Only Sergeant Haydon of 452 Squadron and Casson of 616 Squadron can be said to have definitely fallen to German guns on Circus 68.

Turning now to 616 Squadron, we are confronted by a dichotomy; a squadron that makes the one and only verifiable combat claim for Circus 68, but that has three others "destroyed", with one "probable", all as over-claimed and one loss to friendly fire. Pilot

Officer P W E Nip Heppell, Yellow three, reported as follows:

I was Yellow three when 616 Squadron took off. From the French coast south of Boulogne the squadron went into a left hand orbit. After a few minutes about twenty Me 109s were seen to the east of us and several thousand feet below, climbing up over white cloud. Wing Commander Bader led the squadron into attack in a steep dive. When I got down to their level the enemy aircraft had split up.

I climbed up to the right and saw a 109 F come up in front of me. He appeared to be on the top of a stall turn and so I gave him a long burst closing to point blank range. I saw on the side of his aircraft as he turned to the left a large "6" just behind the cross on the fuselage. He then went into a very slow gliding turn to the left and I had a vivid view of his hood flying off and the pilot jumping out of his machine. I watched him falling and turning over and over until he had dropped down to some low white cloud. His parachute had still not opened so I assume he was killed. His aircraft is claimed as destroyed. The camouflage was a dirty grey and black. In addition to the usual cross there was a "6" behind it. The tail was painted orange and the spinner black and white.

There can be no doubting from this concise and well detailed report that Heppell had shot down Albert Schlager of 3/JG 26, the only German combat loss during Circus 68.

As already noted, Johnnie Johnson saw Schlager's wreckage burning on the ground, and mistakenly believed this to be the Messerschmitt 109 he had shot at. Firing at a Messerschmitt, he had followed as it belched black smoke and went into a steep dive. Hot on its tail, Johnson's intention was to pursue and finish off the aircraft he believed he had just hit, but as he pushed the stick forward his engine cut. It was only as he pulled out that the Merlin engine picked up again, and he saw wreckage burning on the ground near a canal. His belief, incorrectly, was that this was the funeral pyre of the smoke-trailing Messerschmitt he had shot at and which he had followed into its screaming all-out dive. Johnson had, just moments earlier, also fired at another Me 109 with Sergeant Jeff West – the two of them claiming a half share of a Messerschmitt 109 destroyed.

Pilot Officer Roy Marples, evidently the first of the Tangmere Wing to spot the enemy, was flying as Blue three and claimed as "probably destroyed" another Messerschmitt. He had moved in behind a 109 that had broken away – with the intention, he thought, of coming round to attack it from behind. Closing to one hundred and fifty yards, and then down to eighty, he gave him all that he had got in a series of bursts. Although he observed no hits, the enemy continued serenely onwards and downwards in "a power glide" and left

Gp Capt Al Deere, who flew Circus 68 with the Kenley Wing, with his wife Joan at a Buckingham Palace investiture during 1943.

Marples with the impression that the pilot must have been dead otherwise he would have taken evasive action. In fact, Marples was wrong. His shots must all have missed, and the German pilot apparently continued on his way blissfully unaware that he was being shot at.

Sergeant Jeff West, the pugnacious little New Zealander, followed Bader down into the confusion that was about to erupt. Shooting at more than one Messerschmitt 109* he finally went into a spin. Sorting himself out, he again caught sight of what he thought was an enemy aircraft falling and "…which performed strange manoeuvres and adopted remarkable attitudes prior to breaking into pieces." This observation, in the overall context of Bader's last fight, is very significant indeed. We know that Schlager's Messerschmitt did not break into pieces in the air, and we also know that no other German aeroplane was going down at that time. Jeff West can *only* have been witnessing the mid-air break up of his wing leader's Spitfire.

These, then, are the uncomfortable facts emerging from an in-depth look at British combat claims on Circus 68; an operation that saw more Spitfires fall to British guns than to those of the Luftwaffe, where more Spitfires were downed by the RAF than were Messerschmitts, where over-claiming and mis-identification were rife and where the bombing was painfully ineffectual. In a word, it was a shambles. As to the over-claiming aspect, it is interesting to compare the remarks Flight Lieutenant Bill "Hawkeye" Wells made to his colleague "Al" Deere, to Bader's comments (detailed at the beginning of this chapter). Wells was then a flight commander on 485 Squadron in the Kenley Wing who actually flew on Circus 68, as did Deere as CO of 602 Squadron.

Sqn Ldr "Hawkeye" Wells, the CO of 485 Squadron who expressed his concerns to Deere about over-claiming by 452 Squadron.

> Frankly Al, I fail to see how some of the squadrons shoot down the numbers they claim. On a very great number of occasions 485 Squadron has been on the same show, and in the same area of sky, and none of us has seen more than a few stray Messerschmitts. It always mystifies me therefore to find on landing that a particular squadron had destroyed a large number of enemy fighters when we were in spitting distance of that squadron throughout the operation. I have, in fact, reported my beliefs to the station commander.

---

* West's logbook for this operation is endorsed by the squadron intelligence officer, Flying Officer C R Gibbs: "one and a half Me 109 Fs destroyed".

Spitfire P8342 UZ-N of 306 Squadron was flown by Sgt W Jasinski on Circus 68. Here, it is shown with battle damage after landing at Biggin Hill on 29 August 1941 when it was flown by Sgt Machowiak. Clearly, it would not have needed many more hits in the tail section to have caused a catastrophic failure. Unlike Bader, Machowiak had a lucky escape! *(K Choloniewski coll via Matusiak)*

Al Deere goes on to say:

> The question of claims is a difficult one to resolve. Unquestionably, the more experienced a pilot became the more careful he was to weigh the pros and cons of a claim before submitting it as a "destroyed". There must have been many enemy aircraft claimed as "probably destroyed" and others "damaged" when, in fact, they were actually destroyed. Regrettably, the reverse was also true. In most cases, there was no intention on the part of the pilot to mislead; it was more a case of imagination, fired up by the excitement of battle, causing him to dream up a picture in his mind which, in the process of telling, became so real that what started as a probable victory now became an enemy aircraft destroyed. There were, of course, definite cases of exaggeration but the offenders were usually taken to task by their fellow pilots.

The views of these two experienced pilots are significant in the context of this study. We can see that Flight Lieutenant Wells's 485 Squadron made no claims during Circus 68 and in the comments that he made it is clear that he was referring to the other Kenley Wing unit; 452 Squadron. As we have seen, 452 Squadron made no less than five claims on that operation – none of which can be substantiated against German losses. It seems that Wells had a point.

Of course, the focus of this book is about the downing of Douglas Bader but it will not be lost on the reader that the interest surrounding Bader, his last fight and who or what brought him down is due to his uniquely legendary and somewhat iconic status. The fact that friendly fire most likely brought down and killed Sergeant Chapman would be wholly inconsequential to the public at large, the news media, historians or even to television documentary makers. Interest in Sergeant Chapman would hardly have spawned such a flurry of excited enthusiasm as it did for Bader. And yet Chapman had paid the ultimate price.

Chapter Nine

Through Bader's Eyes

As was the case with Albert Schlager and 3/JG 26, nobody on the Tangmere Wing saw the going of Douglas Bader either. At least, nobody *realised* they had seen the going of him. He just vanished and didn't come home. As we know, the version of events published in *Reach for the Sky* explained the downing of his Spitfire to be the result of a mid-air collision with a Messerschmitt 109. However, as already seen in chapter five, there is very clear evidence that his *initial* belief was that he had been shot down. In *Reach for the Sky* the story was told through Paul Brickhill, and it is interesting, therefore, to read Bader's own version of events in the first person. Fortunately, history has left us more than one source for this.

In the immediate post-war period Douglas Bader wrote a piece that saw publication by the North American Newspaper Alliance under the headline: "British Air Ace Describes his Last Trip over France". The article was dated London 3rd December 1945:

Since the idea of an unwilling pilot being attached by one metal leg to a broken Spitfire has caused considerable laughter among some of my friends, I write this story so that others with a similar sense of humour can all have a good laugh:

The Spitfire wing of which I was in charge was located in Sussex. We took off on 9 August 1941. Our target was the neighbourhood of Lille where we met some of our own bombers who were due to blow the daylight out of a French factory. We were well over France when about eighteen Me 109s appeared well below us. Four of us in front dived down onto the leading four German fighters and each took his opposite number. The normal method of making such an attack was to close behind the Me 109, give him a quick squirt and then, from one's superior speed with the dive, pull up and so maintain the height advantage for further attacks.

This time, unfortunately, my judgement was very bad. I nearly collided from behind with my opposite number and I was compelled, instead of pulling up, to go on behind and down underneath him. On getting underneath this collection of Huns I saw, a couple of thousand feet below, and a short distance in front, four more Huns. I thought I might as well have a swing around with them, which I did. As I turned away, I collided with a Me 109 on my right.

It was entirely my fault. The Spitfire's nose dropped very abruptly and the stick and rudder had no feeling in them. The aeroplane was pointing straight downwards and twisting very slowly in a left hand direction. There appeared to be no fuselage behind my seat at all. In fact, the complete tail assembly had been removed.

Immediately I realised I was out of control I cut the engine and the next thing was to get out. The collision took place at about 22,000ft and I started getting out at about 18,000ft. The cockpit hood was a little obstinate before it finally came away. Having undone the harness, I lifted myself up in the seat with my hands to get out. I was surprised to feel as though I was being assisted out of the cockpit. Other pilots who have baled out at high speed have told me there is a kind of suction which helps to pull the pilot out – rather like drawing a cork out of a bottle. Just when everything appeared to be going smoothly and I was nearly clear, I stuck.

The only clear memory is of being held to the aeroplane by my right leg. We parted company at about 4,000ft and I seemed to shoot upwards from the aeroplane, leaving my right leg behind. I released my parachute. Just before passing through a cloud layer about 1,000ft from the ground a Messerschmitt 109 seemed to be rushing towards me…and passed about fifty yards away. The last few hundred feet I remember very clearly, seeing three rustic French figures leaning on a fence beside the field into which I was about to arrive. I do not remember striking the ground because I was knocked out for a couple of minutes. My left leg must have struck me in the chest because I broke two ribs. This, apart from a cut hand and a cut throat was the only damage I suffered.

One point needs explanation. My legs are attached to me by a leather belt around my waist. The right leg which was stuck, I think by the foot somewhere in the top of the cockpit, has a metal arm which slides into the leather belt and is held into position by perfectly normal eyelets done up like a shoe with a lace. This was where the belt broke. The leg went straight out from my trouser leg, making a very neat split the whole way down the inside seam. I do not recall anything between seeing the Frenchmen gaping at me and laying on the ground while three members of the Luftwaffe were removing my parachute harness before carrying me to a car. I was driven, bleeding rather profusely from the throat, to a hospital in St Omer.

Written as it was in 1945, and in the first person, it is perhaps historically more important than the *Reach for the Sky* account. If nothing else it certainly provides us with some extra detail of the event. It was not, though, the first time the collision story had surfaced. As we shall see later, collision was not Bader's first impression, he most certainly believed at the time that he had been shot down.

It was surely more than just a coincidence, then, that one of the first people Bader would write to after being taken into captivity was his old golfing partner, H C Longhurst. Henry Longhurst was a journalist with his own regular column in the *Sunday Times*. It was not the first time that Bader had turned to him to get a story published. Not long after his appointment to the Tangmere Wing, and as a result of Bader's annoyance over problems with runway construction at Tangmere, Longhurst was invited down to Sussex. Here, he was fed a story about the slothful manner in which the runway work was progressing and the apparent disparity in pay and conditions between the workmen and Bader's pilots. Whilst the article was guarded, and did not mention people or places, those "in the know" at the air ministry were left in no doubt! Bader had used the media to his advantage. Now, in captivity, he would do the same.

By October 1941, and quite some while after the British public had been made aware of Bader's captivity, Longhurst first broke the news of the collision in his column, writing:

I have just learned first hand how Wing Commander Douglas Bader DSO and bar, DFC and bar, the legless pilot, managed to get free from his crashing Spitfire and bale out over France last September *(sic)*. It is a remarkable story. He tells it in a letter to me from his prisoner of war camp in Germany.

In one of the sweeps which were an almost daily occurrence at that time he had just destroyed one Messerschmitt when he collided with another. The tail of his aircraft was knocked completely off, and it plunged to earth completely out of control. "I had to jettison my leg," he says "in the somewhat protracted but energetic performance of evacuation. It wished to stay inside a tail-less aeroplane while I wished to leave – so we both had it our own way." How he managed to throw away his right leg I am unable to say, for whenever I have seen him flying he has worn an overall suit with parachute harness attached – completely encasing both his artificial legs.

So, this it would seem was Bader shamelessly exploiting the media through an old friend, purely in order to get his story out into the public domain. Today, it might just be called "spin".

If the collision story first took its roots in the prisoner of war camps, then the testimony of Captain Richard K Page of the Royal Artillery certainly supports this.

Bader's journalist friend and one-time golfing partner, Henry Longhurst, who first broke the news in the British press during 1941 of the mid-air collision with a Messerschmitt 109 over northern France. It was an account which stuck and would ultimately become the accepted version of events that day.

Taken prisoner at Calais on 26 May 1940, Page found himself in Oflag VIB with Bader and it was here that Bader told Page what had happened.

I knew Bader well and shared a small room with him and another RAF officer in our hut at Oflag VIB near Warburg. His version of the shooting down from his own lips was that after a dogfight over France he joined what he thought were 'planes of his own squadron only to realise they had black crosses on their fuselage. He nose-dived out of the formation and in so doing took his tail off on a neighbouring Messerschmitt.

So, a variation on a theme – but a collision story all the same.

During the 1970s, Bader was interviewed for an American aerospace industry magazine called *Code One* by journalist Bob Cunningham. In it, Bader is quoted directly; "I remember I accused Johnnie Johnson and said, 'Well, you probably shot me down. You wanted a promotion...!' I never to this day knew, you know. A fellow could have easily shot me down, and at very close range with cannons, you know, knocked my back end off." It is an illuminating piece. Whilst his comment about Johnson was apparently just a flippant throw-away remark, did it hide something that may have been lurking at the back of his mind?

More significant, though, is the fact that Bader concedes, long after the event, that he could after all have been shot down. It is an important *volte-face* by Bader on the collision story.

Bader also famously appeared on the well-known television programme "This is Your Life" broadcast on 31 March 1982. Hosted by presenter Eamonn Andrews, Bader was reunited with the survivors of A Flight, 616 Squadron, when he jokingly remarked of Jeff West, "I think he shot me down!" Whether or not the remarks about Johnson and West having shot him down were purely jocular they cannot be ignored in the context of this work. The B Flight commander, Squadron Leader L H Casson DFC, who was shot down with Bader on Circus 68 and initially incarcerated with him as a prisoner of war was not invited to participate in the programme.

As for other first-person accounts, there are two more that are somewhat intriguing. The first is Bader's MI9 de-brief questionnaire following his return from captivity. In it, Bader states that he was unwounded when captured although we know that he was certainly injured (cut hand, cut throat and broken ribs). Perhaps Bader was playing with semantics here and considered these were injuries rather than wounds? For whatever reason, though, Bader chose not to mention them in 1945. In itself, this de-brief document perhaps does not add a great deal to our knowledge of events but it certainly adds an interesting perspective. It also confirms the dates and locations of his various PoW camp incarcerations and this, later, is of some significance to the overall story. The next document, though, would be Bader firmly placing into the *official* record the circumstances of how he was downed over France.

Upon his release from Colditz Castle and return to the UK, Bader was promoted to group captain and posted to command the Day Fighter Wing of the Central Fighter Establishment back at his old home – RAF Tangmere. He arrived here in June, and one of the first things he did was to complete retrospectively a combat report for 9 August 1941 (see Appendix B), almost four years after the event. Again, its contents add little to our knowledge of what transpired that day – merely going over the same ground covered in *Reach for the Sky* and Bader's earlier newspaper article. In one respect, though, it is interesting.

In his report he talks of the collision aftermath, stating, "I collided with an Me 109, which took my tail off, it appeared as far up as the radio mast but was actually probably only the empennage." The report carries the stamp of the Intelligence Branch, HQ Fighter Command, where it was received on 17 July 1945. So, pre-dating the *Reach for the Sky* account by nine years, Bader downplayed the assertion that he had lost both tail and fuselage up to the radio mast, suggesting instead that it was probably only the empennage (tail unit) of his Spitfire that had gone.

Perhaps significantly, with regards to how we are to view the introduction of the collision version of events, Douglas Bader's brother-in-law, "Laddie" Lucas, wrote a biography of Bader, *Flying Colours*, which was published in 1981 (during Bader's lifetime) and it is unequivocal in Lucas's forthright view. In it, Lucas puts forward very firmly the view that Bader was shot down. Later, in 1996, Lucas wrote to the *Daily Express* stating:

"For the record, let us be quite clear what befell Douglas Bader on 9 August 1941 over northern France when he was made prisoner of war. Bader was not shot down by anti-aircraft fire as your story of 28 January suggests, nor was his loss the result of a mid-air collision.

GENERAL QUESTIONNAIRE. PART II. TOP SECRET.
TOP SECRET
M.I.9/Gen/
MIS-X

RANK   SURNAME

N NAMES

Capture:
d in your unit on how to behave in the event of capture?
en and by whom?

No

d on escape and evasion? (State where, when and by whom).

No

er capture:
gated by the enemy? (State where, when and methods employed by enemy).

d partly successful escape? (Give details of each attempt separately, stating where,
, names of your companions, where and when recaptured and by whom. Were you

struction of enemy factory plant, war material, communications, etc., when employed
escape? (Give details, places and dates.)

No

uy:
American personnel who collaborated with the enemy or in any way helped the
isoners of War? (Give details, names of person(s) concerned, camp(s), dates
help given to enemy.)

ence of bad treatment by the enemy to yourself or to others, or knowledge of
Convention you should ask for a copy of "Form Q" on which to make your

n inviting information on "War Crimes" and describes the kinds of offences.

PART I
TOP SECRET
M.I.9/Gen/
MIS-X

GENERAL QUESTIONNAIRE FOR BRITISH/AMERICAN EX-PRISONERS OF WAR

1. No. 26151   RANK Wg Commander   SURNAME BADER
   CHRISTIAN NAMES DOUGLAS ROBERT STEWART
   DECORATIONS D.S.O. D.F.C.

2. SHIP (R.N., U.S.N. or MERCHANT NAVY)
   UNIT (ARMY)
   SQUADRON (R.A.F. or A.A.F.) 11 Group. TANGMERE. WING.

3. DIVISION (ARMY), COMMAND (R.A.F. or A.A.F.) 11 Group

4. DATE OF BIRTH   21/2/1910

5. DATE OF ENLISTMENT   Nov '39.

6. CIVILIAN TRADE OR PROFESSION
   (OR EXAMINATIONS PASSED WHILE P/W)

7. PRIVATE ADDRESS   RED WELLS, ASCOT, BERKSHIRE

8. PLACE AND DATE OF ORIGINAL CAPTURE   St OMER. FRANCE. 9/8/41.

9. WERE YOU WOUNDED WHEN CAPTURED?   No.

10. MAIN CAMPS OR HOSPITALS IN WHICH IMPRISONED.

Camp No.	Location	From	Till
DULAG LUFT.	FRANKFURT-MAIN.	11 Aug 41	28 Aug 41
7 C.	LUBECK	30 Aug 41	1 Oct 41
VI B.	WARBURG.	Oct 41	11 Aug 42
LUFT III.	SAGAN.	13 Aug 42	? Jul 42
VIII B	(LAMSDORF)	30 Jul 42	18 Aug 42
IV C.	COLDITZ	Aug 42	15 Apr 45

11. WERE YOU IN A WORKING CAMP?   YES.

Location	From	Till	Nature of Work
GLEIWITZ	2/8/42 ?	7/8/42 ?	

Escaped in working party till e little to
getaway aeroplane. Failed.

12. DID YOU SUFFER FROM ANY SERIOUS ILLNESSES WHILE A P/W?

Nature of Illness	Cause	Duration

No.

(3) DID YOU RECEIVE ADEQUATE MEDICAL TREATMENT?

Not NECESSARY.

SECURITY UNDERTAKING.

I fully realise that all information relating to the matters covered by the questions in Part II.
are of a highly secret and official nature.
I have had explained to me and fully understand that under Defence Regulations or
U.S.A.R. 380-5 I am forbidden to publish or communicate any information concerning
these matters.

Date   19 Apr 45.   Signature   DRS Bader.

The MI9 Prisoner of War de-brief questionnaire filled out by Bader on his return from Colditz Castle. MI9 were responsible for all aspects of RAF aircrew escape and evasion. *(National Archives)*

Lucas goes on to express Galland's emphatic view that Bader was most definitely shot down, with Lucas identifying the victor as an Oberfeldwebel Max Mayer of 6/JG 26. In fact, it was a Walter Meyer of JG 26 who was involved in the combat that day. Max Mayer was an imposter who had contacted Bader during 1981 saying that he was the man who had shot him down. Walter Meyer, the real Luftwaffe fighter pilot, had died during 1943. The charlatan Max Mayer was a fantasist who can be completely dismissed from the equation.

Thus far we have seen how the circumstances surrounding the loss of Douglas Bader into captivity had been perceived (both officially and unofficially) from the British side, and how Bader himself portrayed these events. How the Germans viewed the event is looked at in chapter eleven, but first we need to examine the circumstances, so far as they are known, relating to Bader's landing by parachute and his subsequent capture.

Chapter Ten

Bader's Landing, Capture and Imprisonment

When undertaking the research into the last fight of Douglas Bader, and trying to make sense of all the known facts, it was important to establish the place where Bader had landed by parachute. The intention, when undertaking this work, was to look at every detail that could be turned up – including the very minutiae of the day if it could be found. Fortunately, and as one might imagine with such a notable arrival on French soil, there were those who knew well the exact place of his landing.

The descent of an English pilot minus one leg was something that quite understandably stuck in the mind of fourteen-year-old Arthur Dubreu, who was able to pinpoint the location of his landing in a meadow behind the farm of Florent May (now Ferme St Omer), between Boeseghem and Blaringhem, and approximately ten kilometres to the south-east of St Omer. Dubreu, in 2005, was adamant that this was the landing place of Bader. Others, too, who lived in the locality, were sure that this was where Bader had landed and there was also an account that Bader had been helped to the lane nearby, Rue Basse. They said he had been helped by farmer Florent May and another local resident, although an eighteen-year-old garage mechanic from Blaringhem, Pierre Bernard, had been the first to help Bader after he landed. Reputedly, it was not until Bernard saw the film *Reach for the Sky* in 1965 that he realised whom he had helped!

Here, outside 25 Rue Basse, a chair was apparently found for the airman from an adjacent cottage whilst the arrival of the German military was awaited and he was eventually taken away by car. (Interestingly, this location is just a little over one kilometre away from the crash site of Albert Schlager's Messerschmitt 109.) The question as to where Douglas Bader's Spitfire had fallen had yet to be answered, although retired meteorological office senior forecaster, Jim Allen, came up with a detailed calculation which worked back from Bader's reported landing site, tracked his path of descent across the ground and also estimated on the map his approximate point of exit from the stricken Spitfire. (See map page 94) Factored into this calculation were the average rates of descent for a GQ or Irvin parachute of the type Bader would have been using and also his estimated body weight at the time. It was a fascinating exercise, made possible by surviving British and German weather reports for the day, and one which would later have some significance in relation to the supposed crash location.

Once Bader was taken away, he was driven to the Clinique Sterin, a hospital by the junction of Rue des Pipiers and Rue Saint-Bertin, St Omer, which in time of war had become a Luftwaffe hospital. The story of Bader's initial incarceration at the Clinique is recorded in *Reach for the Sky*. It was here, in hospital, and not many days after his arrival that Bader was visited by Luftwaffe personnel who eventually were able to reunite him with his rather battered artificial right leg. It had been found by a French civilian, Georges Jourdain, laying in a field near Route Nationale 43 between Racquinghem and Wittes – and not buried beneath the wreckage of Bader's Spitfire as suggested in *Reach for the Sky*.

The hospital at St Omer, the Clinique Sterin, from where Bader escaped whilst being treated. Despite its normal wartime use as a Luftwaffe hospital it frequently received wounded RAF aircrew prisoners from the region. This photo was taken during July 2007 when demolition work had just commenced at the rear.

Jourdain had handed his somewhat bizarre and puzzling discovery to the Gendarmes and they, in turn, had passed it over to the German authorities. Incredibly, and unknown to Jim Allen when he made his meteorologically based scientific calculations, the reported position where the artificial leg was found was almost exactly at the cross on the map where Allen had calculated Bader must have exited his Spitfire to begin his parachute descent.

With the leg battered and bent, Bader made a request that an attempt be made by the Luftwaffe to effect some running repairs. The Luftwaffe were evidently only too pleased to oblige, but Bader also requested that a message be got back to England requesting a replacement right leg. Again, the Germans were only too happy to help and at 11.34 on 13 August 1941 North Foreland radio picked up a broadcast from Ushant stating that Bader was prisoner but had lost his right artificial leg in a parachute jump. A request for a replacement leg was made, with the Germans offering safe passage to the delivering aircraft. Thus, four days after he was brought down, came the first confirmation for the RAF that he was, at least, alive.

The leg, when it came, was packed into a specially made wooden crate and delivered during the course of Circus 81 by Blenheim R3843 of 18 Squadron, crewed by Sergeants Nickleson, Meadows and Pearson, over what they believed was the south-west corner of St Omer-Longuenesse airfield. The box was jettisoned at 10.57 from 10,000ft and photographed by Nickleson during its descent. The safe conduct offer made by the Germans had not been accepted *per-se*. Instead, the leg was delivered during a routine operation and fell near Quiestède, the puzzling object watched in its gentle but flak-punctuated descent by villagers Maurice Delvart, Gisele Delpouve and Simone Berquer – the latter noticing clearly, as the box was carried off by the Germans, that it was marked with the Red Cross symbol. Simone, puzzled, wondered why the RAF were now dropping humanitarian aid to the enemy.

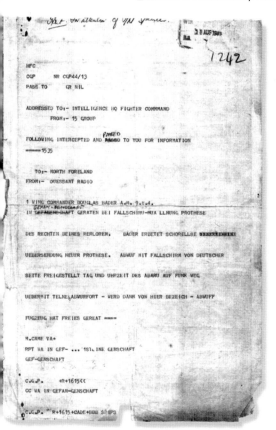

At the St Omer hospital Bader found himself in the company of other wounded and injured RAF fighter pilots. Amongst them, an American flier Pilot Officer W T "Bill" Hall, downed on 2 July whilst flying Circus 29 in a 71 Squadron Hurricane and who had become the first Eagle Squadron prisoner of war. Hall, a likeable and irrepressible former Alaskan bush pilot, had been undergoing treatment for a severe wound to a kneecap. Also there, just ahead of Bader, was Pilot Officer Justin O'Byrne of 452 Squadron, like Bader, another casualty of Circus 68. Justin O'Byrne was a tough and rugged Australian from Tasmania – a sheep station manager in his pre-war life. He joined Hall in a small ward, along with a Polish pilot who was said to be a veteran of

The teleprinter message to the intelligence section of HQ Fighter Command on 13 August 1941 with the first indication that Bader was safe. For a translation see Appendix L. The original of this document is in the author's collection, but another copy of the same document was sold at auction by Sotheby's in November 1995 for £5,750.00 to the family of Sir Alan Smith, Bader's usual number two.

The crew of the delivering aircraft. L to R: Sgt John Nickleson (pilot), Sgt Walter Meadows (observer) and Sgt John Pearson (wireless operator/air gunner). All three crew were lost in R3843 on 20 September 1941 during an attack on shipping off the Dutch coast.

The casket containing the spare artificial leg for Bader after being picked up near St Omer. It appears to have been attached to a standard RAF seat-type parachute and the difficulties associated with throwing out the case and an already open parachute into the slipstream of the delivering Blenheim must have been enormous. *(RAF Museum)*

France and the Battle of Britain and who had been badly burned around the face and hands when shot down.

This was Pilot Officer Wladyslaw Chciuk of 308 Squadron who had been shot down on a Circus operation on 24 July 1941. In *Reach for the Sky* mention is made of Bill Hall and the Pole, and also of a Londoner called "Willie" (also said to be a Spitfire pilot) who is described as having been shot through the mouth. Thus far it has been impossible to identify the pilot Bader called Willie and, in his contemporary hand-written account, O'Byrne talks *only* of Hall, the Pole, Bader and himself being in the ward. He makes no mention at all of the mysterious Willie in his detailed account.

O'Byrne goes on to describe how the three of them hatched an escape plot, with the collusion of one of the French nurses, and planned to make a rope from knotted bed sheets and blankets, but that he and the Pole were moved to Germany just before they could execute the escape attempt. Oddly, and especially given the fact that O'Byrne was another victim of Circus 68, Bader makes no reference to him being at Clinique Sterin in *Reach for the Sky*. Instead, he is replaced in the account with another, seemingly fictitious, prisoner of war Spitfire pilot – the aforementioned Willie.

In *Reach for the Sky* we have Bader suddenly alighting on the bed-sheet idea himself *after* the Pole and Willie had been moved from St Omer Hospital to a prisoner of war camp in Germany. In reality, though, we know from O'Byrne's testimony that it was a plan hatched jointly by the four captive pilots. Certainly, we know from O'Byrne's MI9 post captivity de-brief document that he was at the St Omer hospital up until 20 August 1941 (when he arrived at Dulag Luft, Frankfurt) recovering from cannon shrapnel wounds to his ankle and Achilles tendon. Chciuk had been moved some time earlier, on 14 August it would seem. As is well recorded, we know that Bader was entertained by Galland and his men during his hospital sojourn at St Omer.

This was at Audembert airfield (not Wissant as stated in *Reach for the Sky*) and from the Propaganda Kompanie report concerning Ober-leutnant Schmid (chapter five) we know that Bader's visit to JG 26 had certainly taken place at some date immediately prior to 24 August, the date of the PK report. Given that Bader says he made his now famous escape attempt from the St Omer clinic the night immediately following his visit to Galland, and since we know from the German Army signal that Bader had fled the St Omer clinic on the night of 18/19 August, we can be certain that Bader's visit to Galland was on 18 August 1941.

According to Bader's testimony, he was shown his newly delivered spare artificial leg the same evening he was recaptured and we know this was dropped by parachute in the area of Quiestède (approximately

Plt Off Wladyslaw Chciuk, one of the pilots who shared the small hospital ward at St Omer with Bader.

eight kilometres south-east of St Omer) on 19 August 1941. Taken to Clairmarais airfield (occupied by JG 26), the leg was photographed there by the Germans outside their aerodrome control building, a requisitioned farm property situated on the aerodrome's northern boundary. Still there today, the building is just about unchanged but is now in use as a hunting lodge and retains a good deal of evidence of its former Luftwaffe usage – including the watch office and its improvised window overlooking the flying field. Most likely it was to this building that the newly recaptured Bader was brought on the evening of 19 August, and it was probably here that Bader spent a hot and uncomfortable night in an upstairs room before being taken off to Germany. It is possible, therefore, to establish with confidence a time-line from Bader's capture on 9 August up until his transfer to the Frankfurt Dulag Luft reception and interrogation centre for air force prisoners.

Bader's later captivity is not something with which this book is concerned in any detail. However, of his hospitalisation and later imprisonment (as described in *Reach for the Sky*) there is a certain amount of peculiarity. In the book, and through Brickhill, Bader details his initial camp as Oflag VIB at Warburg telling how a few of the inmates were RAF although "he knew none of them". In fact, that is most certainly not the case. Also incarcerated at VIB over the same period was Justin O'Byrne – his very recent hospital ward-mate at St Omer! Also in the same camp there was another significant Circus 68 player, Flight Lieutenant Buck Casson.

The rear of the building showing the room from which Bader escaped down a rope of knotted bed sheets. This photograph was said to have been sent to Bader post-war by a German and shows the improvised rope. Closer examination of the photograph seems to suggest that the rope has, in fact, been painted onto the image!

In the case of Buck we absolutely know that he met there with Bader since his communication to him of May 1945 began with the words: "Dear Douglas, Many thanks for your letter and I hope you are as full of vigour as you were when I last saw you at VIB." Later, and when writing in August 1995, Casson re-confirmed his presence in the same camp, stating: "Douglas Bader arrived there and I saw quite a bit of him until everyone was moved out to Schubin." Odd, then, that Bader should deny he knew anyone at that camp. Curious, too, that he should fail to

The same view, July 2007. The rear elevation of the now abandoned Clinique Sterin has been altered by a post-war block to the right and a fire escape from what was the window at the top left. Bader's small ward was the second window along from the fire escape exit. Identifying features of the building can be picked out in both the period photograph and the more recent image.

mention O'Byrne – either at St Omer or of him being in Oflag VIB. Strange, also, that Bader should fail to mention Casson *anywhere* in *Reach for the Sky* – particularly since Casson was a key member of 616 Squadron and the Tangmere Wing and was also downed on the same operation. Quite apart from the omission of what one might reasonably consider significant detail, much of Bader's tale seems to be somewhat flawed in its accuracy when one delves not too far beneath the surface. Unravelling the true story continually seems to pose more questions than it answers.

Luftwaffe personnel of JG 26 inspect Bader's newly delivered spare leg at St Omer-Clairmarais, August 1941. *(RAF Museum)*

CHAPTER ELEVEN

THE GERMAN PERSPECTIVE

From the German point of view, things were somewhat different to how Bader had viewed his arrival in France. There was no collision. Of that much the official German records and the account of Adolf Galland in his book *The First and the Last* both agree. Indeed, in the 1977 interview with the author, Galland was absolutely adamant. Bader had been shot down.

> The problem was that we didn't know who by. It was all very odd. You must understand that we in the Luftwaffe had very strict rules for the confirmation of "kills". Exact times and places, witnesses, wreckage on the ground – that sort of thing – all had to match up. All the facts were looked at in detail before a pilot was granted the victory. Now, with Bader of course, we all wanted to have been the one who had shot him down. You can be sure of that. Imagine the fame that the deed would bring the pilot and what the propaganda people could make of it. The fact is we looked very carefully to see who might have been the pilot concerned but couldn't find one.

> There were several Spitfires down that day but these kills were all tied into specific pilots. But not the wing commander's Spitfire. I think we looked at Leutnant Kosse as a possible victor but the facts of his "kill" didn't fit either. It would have been nice if we could have fitted a pilot's name to Bader's victory and we even looked to see if it might have been the one pilot we lost that day *(Schlager)* but it wasn't him. I don't remember now why it couldn't have been him, but it wasn't. To be truthful, I just cannot understand why we couldn't find out despite trying very hard. It really is quite strange.

Surprisingly, perhaps, the Germans seem to have made little or no propaganda capital out of the capture of Douglas Bader although they knew full well that he was a household name in Britain. In fact, it can only be said that they acted entirely honourably – and with considerable compassion and humanity – not only in sending a wireless transmission saying that Bader had been captured, but in offering safe passage to an RAF aircraft for the delivery of his spare leg. There is no reason at all to suppose that the Germans would not have honoured their offered gesture, and one can understand their dismay when the leg was eventually "delivered" in the course of a bombing raid.

Before the leg drop, of course, Bader had been entertained by Galland and JG 26. Again, this was not covered in the German press although this can be explained, quite simply, by

Bader is entertained by Galland and selected officers of JG 26 at La Colombier, Audembert. Johannes Schmid, who was introduced as Bader's victor, is fourth from the left in a light coloured flying jacket, just over Galland's right shoulder. *(via Caldwell)*

Bader takes his leave of Galland and his men at Audembert before being driven back to hospital at St Omer from where he almost immediately escaped. *(via M Booker)*

the fact that no warring nation wants to "humanise" its enemy. Exposure of the Galland/Bader meeting in the press would have done just that. In addition, media exposure of individual prisoners of war was forbidden under the Geneva Convention and the Germans were apparently intent on respecting that particular obligation in this instance.

We have already looked at Galland's perception of these events in his book *The First and the Last*, but there are other aspects of the German perspective to look at. Although it must be taken for what it is, the report of war correspondent Hans Kreten on the events of 9 August 1941 gives an interesting insight:

Today, Saturday, the RAF continued its attempts to fly into the occupied French area and again we experienced the same thing that we so often experienced in the last week: the attack was a heavy defeat for the RAF. The propaganda success of this offensive, which the British at least promised, will however be made apparent after this defeat.

The daily work of our fighter groups is hard and exciting here in our aerodromes. Planes are improved, overhauled, and new machines are ready to fly. Small damage must be repaired in the shortest time. This requires much hard work and restlessness for the men who must still remain at a state of readiness. But when Tommy comes, our fighters are there and prepare for him a hellish dance in the skies. If he also entrusts his bomber groups with just as strong a fighter protection then they must pay tribute to our own defences.

Misty weather gives the advantage to the first larger incoming flight of the Tommies in the midday hours of today. *(Circus 68 – Author)*

For our fighters, as for the flak, the defence was made more difficult. For the attackers, however, the weather report was very advantageous. And nevertheless, our fighters found and laid into the enemy. And again we saw, as far as the weather permitted, the well known picture of the aerial battles. And then the moment came when our fighters returned over the aerodrome, sweeping overhead, engines howling and wings waggling: they had pounded the Tommy again. And still he came in another attack after mid-day but with stronger groups. The clearer weather soon brought fighters to the enemy and once again Tommy had to suffer the attack with bitter losses. In total today thirteen British aeroplanes were downed over French soil and into the Channel. Galland shot down his 75th opponent in the course of today's battle with unmatchable mastery.

In another bitter combat, Hauptmann Schoepfel, commander of a fighter group, gained his 33rd victory. After he had shot all his munitions in a seemingly ever expanding air battle he hit the engine of a Tommy with his last shot. It made escape impossible and he was forced to make a landing on French soil. The British pilot, a captain, got out of his aircraft after the landing and greeted his circling victor with a wave and then set his wreck alight. A few days beforehand, Hauptmann Schoepfel shot down an English fighter when the Tommy struck a roof truss.

This weekend's visit of the RAF to our fighters on the Channel brought the second biggest blow, with the Tommies losing forty-one machines in our sector of the front. If the RAF continue their offensive attempts as they currently are then our Luftwaffe will fight back obliterating them. This was clearly proven once again this week here on the Channel.

Setting aside for one moment the fact that this was a piece for German public consumption that had been written by a Propaganda Kompanie journalist, it does contain a certain amount of indisputable factual information: the weather, the midday attack, the later RAF operations, Galland's victory, the circumstances of Schoepfel's claim, Casson's downing etc. Yet it makes no mention of the capture of the famous British flier, Bader. In fact, with regards to the overall success figures they give, the German claims are not *too* wildly out. A total of thirteen claimed destroyed against eleven RAF fighters lost that day can hardly be described as wild exaggeration on the part of the Luftwaffe: In fact in the week thirty RAF fighters and three RAF bombers were lost in the Channel/northern France area of operations and forty-one were *claimed* by the Germans. This is hardly extreme exaggeration – especially given the claims being made by the RAF over the same time span. All in all, it is easy to imagine this self-same war correspondent's report being written in exactly the same style to cover the British angle on things. The same story, but painted a different colour with another brush. In fact, British newspapers of the period were filled with similar writings, extolling the prowess of Britain's fighting forces and their undoubted superiority over the enemy. This is just the way of things in war, and if the *Berliner Zeitung* had been giving its account of Circus 68 and the numbers of the enemy who had been vanquished, then so too would the *Daily Express* in London. For both the German and British press it was a case of merely reporting the "facts" fed to them by the relevant military propaganda machines. In Britain, the details of air force operations emanated from the air ministry but were supplied

Bader centre stage again and back at Tangmere, this time commanding the Day Fighter Wing in the summer of 1945.

to the news industry through the ministry of information. In this way, the details of "kill" scores fed up the chain from squadron intelligence officer level percolated out into the newspapers. Consequently, over-claiming (on both the German and British sides) helped to feed the propaganda machine and boost public morale. The reality was that it was not necessarily in the interests of either warring nation to pare down the scores to more realistic levels – even if it had been possible to do so. Undoubtedly, the most famous example of over inflated claims in British newspapers came on 16 September 1940 when they reported resounding successes on 15 September, "Battle of Britain day". Headlines trumpeted "185 Shot Down". The real figure was found to be nearer sixty. There were, however, additional angles to Germany's take on things other than just their news reports.

A valuable source of daily tactical information on German operations came from Britain's "Y" Service, a listening organisation that monitored all German wireless transmissions and broadcasts. This organisation was part of the RAF and came under the wing of the AI4 (Air Intelligence 4) department and the information gathered sometimes enabled decisions to be made that would affect immediate combat situations. In the case of Circus 68, a number of German radio transmissions were followed, and although we unfortunately do not have surviving transcripts of German radio chatter like that from the Beachy Head station we do have the report from Group Captain L F Blandy, dated 10 August 1941, which gave a broad-brush picture of events gleaned by the Y Service the previous day:

"Area of Operation: Dunkirk – Le Touquet. 24 aircraft heard.

At 11.11 an auxiliary force (sic) of British aircraft was reported near Le Touquet flying East at 9000 metres. A minute later a flight of British aircraft was approaching

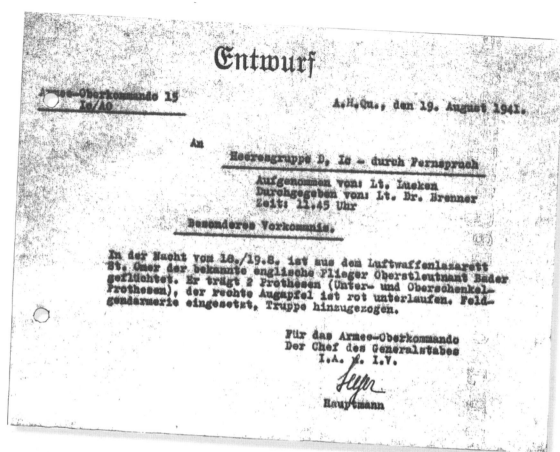

The German Special Notice.

Dunkirk from the north-west at 2,000 metres. The main British force was following at 4,000 metres. At 11.18 a force of British aircraft was flying in a northerly direction over St Omer at heights up to 11,000 metres. At 11.20 British aircraft were reported 15 kilometres south of Dunkirk at 4,500 metres still flying south-east. Yet another flight of British aircraft was reported to have crossed the coast to the west of Dunkirk at 11.28 flying south. At 11.34 the aircraft were south-west of St Omer. A minute later reference is made to a parachute. It is uncertain however whether this parachute came from a British aircraft. At 11.37 the British aircraft were reported to be flying back in a north-westerly direction and the position of German aircraft at 11.38 was over Calais, height between 300 and 2,000 metres. At 11.39 another flight of British aircraft flew out to the west of Dunkirk. At 11.47 three Spitfires were reported over Le Touquet at 2,000 metres. At 11.55 all British aircraft were reported to have gone home. German aircraft, however, appear to have followed British aircraft to Margate as they gave the position of the British at 11.58 as 5 kilometres off Margate."

It is possible that the parachute reported at 11.35 was that of 452 Squadron's Sergeant Haydon (downed a little before then according to German combat reports) and the German transmission about this event may well have been chatter between Oberleutnant Schmid and Unteroffizier Richter. Reference to a descending parachute in German combat reports only appears in that relating to Schmid's victory, who was almost certainly Haydon. No other reference to descending parachutes that might have been Bader or O'Byrne seems to appear in transmissions by the Luftwaffe, but if those two RAF pilots *did* fall to friendly fire then it is quite possible that they would not have been seen by German fliers.

It is also illuminating to look at the German special notice from A H Qu (Army Headquarters) of Oberkommando 15 of 19 August 1941. In it, it is reported that Oberstleutnant Bader had escaped during the night of 18/19 August 1941 from the Luftwaffe hospital at St Omer. He was, it is reported, fitted with two artificial legs and had a severely bloodshot right eye. This German notice is significant as it firmly dates Bader's escape. Rather more interesting is the information that Bader's right eye was still badly bloodshot, a full ten days after his bale out (See chapter fifteen).

Before leaving this chapter on the German perspective we return again to Adolf Galland who, during the summer of 1945, was brought as prisoner of war to RAF Tangmere to be interviewed by RAF pilots at the fighter leader's school. By an incredible reversal of fortunes, Bader was now back at Tangmere and it was here that he met Galland again for the first time since the tea party at Les Colombiers, Audembert.

In the interview with the author in 1977, Galland said that Bader did not exactly reciprocate the same level of hospitality that he had so willingly extended to him in 1941. To be fair to Bader, though, he had most likely been embittered by four long years of unpleasant incarceration – some of it spent in the notorious Colditz Castle. On the other hand, Luftwaffe fighter ace Gunther Rall was also brought to Tangmere with Galland. Rall remembers the kindness shown to the prisoners by the RAF pilots there and, according to Rall, one of the prisoners was the Ju 87 "Stuka" ace Hans-Ulrich Rudel who had lost the lower part of his leg towards the end of the war. He arrived at Tangmere on crutches, hobbling out of the RAF aircraft that had brought him to the airfield there with his artificial limb sticking out of his rucksack. Bader, no doubt feeling an empathy with this fellow amputee pilot-prisoner, reportedly arranged for an orthopaedic surgeon to travel down from London to measure and fit Rudel with a modern aluminium prosthesis. So, if Bader did not "repay" Galland's hospitality he did, apparently, remember the debt he still owed the Luftwaffe for initially fixing his damaged leg and then arranging for the delivery of its replacement.

Whatever the German view, or the British perspective for that matter, it was still a case of piecing together all the available bits of the jigsaw puzzle to complete the picture. The pursuit of Bader's Spitfire, W3185, was the next step.

Chapter Twelve

The Hunt for Spitfire W3185

The Spitfire in which Wing Commander Douglas Bader had been flying when brought down over France on 9 August 1941 was his own "personalised" aeroplane, a Mk VA. By this stage in the war Spitfire squadrons were being re-equipped with the cannon-armed Spifire Mk VBs, but Bader was very anti-cannon and was adamant about his preferences. Consequently, he sought out and was allocated a Mk VA which was equipped with the standard armament of eight .303 machine guns as fitted to the earlier Mk I and II Spitfires.

W3185 was a Vickers Armstrong built airframe, and was a "presentation" Spitfire bearing the name "Lord Lloyd". It was accepted by 39 Maintenance Unit on 11 May 1941 before delivery to 145 Squadron on 30 June. At that time, 145 Squadron formed part of the Tangmere Wing but were replaced in the wing by 41 Squadron during July 1941 when W3185 was nominally transferred to 41 Squadron on the 29th of that month. On the same day it was then re-allocated, this time to the strength of 616 Squadron. The reason is clear. Bader's preference was not only for a machine-gun-armed Spitfire but also to fly with 616 Squadron.

Consequently, this Spitfire Mk VA was "sourced" for the wing leader from one of the other wing squadrons and, for maintenance purposes, it was put onto 616 Squadron's books. It did not, however, carry the identification code YQ as worn by all 616 Squadron Spitfires at that time. Instead, it followed the newly adopted convention of wing leader's aeroplanes wearing the initials of the pilot concerned. In this case, W3185 predictably wore the initials DB on the fuselage sides.

Inevitably, and with what is now an almost global interest in the search for memorabilia of the 1939-45 air war, it was not going to be too long before attention was turned towards hunting for the wreck of Bader's Spitfire. After all, he was one of the best known fighter pilots of WW2 and the circumstances of the incident suggested that the crash site may well yield tangible relics of this iconic pilot's aeroplane. It was well recorded that he had been lost in the general area of St Omer and this, at least, would provide a starting point for any search. Unfortunately, though, the German occupation had meant that civilian records such as civil defence or police reports on air crashes either did not survive, were patchy and incomplete or were not even made at the time. After all, these were military incidents and were of primary interest to the occupying military force, and not particularly the affair of the local civilian authorities. By and large, this was the situation across most of occupied France.

Searching for a specific aircraft crash site, therefore, can be like looking for a needle in the proverbial haystack. Certainly, there are still living witnesses to be found in France during the early days of the twenty-first century who can vividly remember wartime events. Very often, though, the passage of time has muddled or confused the facts in the minds of those who were there. Not only that, but the sheer number of such incidents sometimes tended to blur one story into another. In the Pas de Calais alone there were quite literally hundreds of wartime RAF fighter crashes. Very often, though, a clue to the location of a particular site might be through the burial location of the pilot if he was a casualty. In the case of Bader, of course, there was not such a link. The only clue to work from was "somewhere near St Omer", and that is a big chunk of country to use as a starting point.

During 1982, however, the author put out tentative feelers in the St Omer/Béthune areas of France and published appeals in the local newspaper *Voix du Nord* and *Nord Littoral* and via the mayors of Béthune, St Omer and Aire-sur-la-Lys. All of these enquiries drew blanks in relation to any definite "fix" on Bader's crash site, but a number of correspondents knew of other wartime air crashes although none looked promising in relation to Circus 68. Indeed, at this stage there was not even a vestige of a clue as to where the Spitfire might have fallen other than that it was probably not too far from St Omer. It was a big haystack and a very small needle.

For the time being, at least, the project was put to bed by both researchers and searchers in the UK after 1985 – although French enthusiasts J P Duriez and Jocelyn Leclerc, who had also been looking, continued to chase up leads. By 1996, however, UK-based researcher and writer Dilip Sarkar of the Malvern Spitfire Team got back on the track of looking for the Bader Spitfire. The hunt was charted in the British press who followed the story with enthusiasm, *The Daily Telegraph* of 28 January 1996 claiming in the headline of a piece by Harry Pugh and Tim Reid: "Douglas Bader's Spitfire found in French Field". According to the article, Dilip had located the wreckage buried at its crash site near St Omer and planned to recover the remains later that same year. As it transpired they were extravagant claims based upon the flimsiest of evidence.

On 16 May that year, *The Times* was able to report on the eventual excavation of the crash site by Dilip and his team under the headline: "Is this the grave of Bader's missing Spitfire?" The sub heading was, "Aircraft hunters hail find of wreckage buried under 15 feet of French mud". The article was published with photographs of the "dig" underway and another of Lady Joan Bader holding one of the recovered propeller blades. The question posed in the headline of the article, though, was well founded. As it turned out, the wreckage recovered was that of a Mk IX Spitfire that had crashed at Les Clies, just to the north of Boeseghem, and said to have been lost there during 1943. Its pilot, according to the Malvern Spitfire Team subsequently, had been 27-year-old Squadron Leader Phillip Archer of 421 Squadron, RCAF, who hailed from Hastings, Barbados, and was lost on 17 June 1943. He now lies buried in Longuenesse Cemetery, St Omer.

The article in *The Times* suggested that the recovered aeroplane may well have been Bader's, but left a question mark hanging over the matter, stating that the wreck recovery team were "almost certain" they had found the right aeroplane. The reality, though, was that the team already knew from their excavation that this was a cannon-armed Mk IX Spitfire with a Rolls-Royce Merlin 66 rather than a 45 engine and fitted with a four-bladed propeller rather than a three blader. Not only that, but a wristwatch and pilot's parachute "D"-ring were found in the wreckage, clearly indicative of the pilot having been killed in the crash and thus ruling out Bader on that evidence alone.

French researcher, Hugues Chevalier, is adamant that the recovery team allowed "doubt to hover" with the newspapers, and that according to him they had "concealed the truth by hiding away all 20mm munitions" that had been found there, although one round (dated 1942) was found at the dig site by a local resident, Monsieur Mametz. Whatever the truth behind the 1996 dig, the Malvern team had been fully justified in initially pursuing the excavation at the absolute insistence of Arthur Dubreu and Georges Goblet that this was the Bader crash site. However, when faced with the reality that the recovered Spitfire wreckage was not Bader's machine after all, the Malvern team was anxious to identify which aeroplane and pilot was in fact linked to their recovery.

Ironically, the Malvern team fell into the same trap as Dubreu and Goblet by drawing incorrect conclusions about the identity of

Sqn Ldr Philip Archer DFC.

this aeroplane and pilot. In the case of the Spitfire wreck they had recovered, and with only circumstantial evidence and no hard facts on which to base such a conclusion, they pronounced that they had ascertained the wreck to be that of Spitfire LZ996 flown by Squadron Leader Philip Archer DFC. It wasn't. Surviving RAF casualty records, based upon the post-war work of the Missing Research & Enquiry Unit, clearly record that Squadron Leader Archer was killed when Spitfire LZ996 crashed into a field at Alquines to the west of Lumbres. This is some forty kilometres from the site excavated by the Malvern team. Their inaccurate assumption has been perpetuated, at least twice since that excavation, in published material. All that can be determined is that the excavated Spitfire was, apparently, a Mk IX and that its pilot had perished in the crash. Also, that it was equipped with a Rolls-Royce Merlin 61, whereas LZ996 had been delivered with a Merlin 63. Either way, it wasn't W3185. The question remained; where was Bader's Spitfire?

A French enthusiast and researcher, Joss Leclerc, reckoned he had a lead and had identified a likely crash site as being Bader's and duly notified Dilip of his findings. This "new" site was situated at Mont Dupil on the N43 between Racquinghem and Wittes. Again, the evidence was inconclusive, but a local newspaper report he had traced from 1945 spoke about the crash and told of the pilot landing at Boeseghem. In January 1945 the newspaper *L'Echo de la Lys* reported a 1943 wartime incident near Mont Dupil, and ended that particular story by stating:

> Finally, it should be mentioned that some time earlier a British aircraft had crashed in a field adjoining the farm of Charles Duhamel; the pilot was saved by his parachute and landed at Rue Basse in Boeseghem.

It was a significant and very important linking of the Mont Dupil crash to the parachutist at Rue Basse, and is the nearest the author has been able to get to any contemporary record of the event.

The farmer at Mont Dupil (Charles Duhamel's son) reportedly dated the incident for Leclerc as sometime during 1941. Tenuous though they were, the facts all seemed to fit. Consequently, Dilip excavated the general location identified for him at Mont Dupil during August of 1996, but no trace of aircraft wreckage could be found. The trail had gone cold. The needle was still in the haystack.

By 2004 the author had again become interested in the possibility of finding the Bader crash site, and this interest had been strengthened by a resumption in his research into the overall picture of 9 August 1941. In fact, the letter from Buck Casson to the author on 12 February 1990, which had enclosed a copy of the May 1945 letter to Bader, had always raised a number of questions. Eventually, taking the bull very firmly by the horns, those questions were put by the author to Casson in a letter of 10 January 2001:

> Looking back on our correspondence I have found your letter in which you enclosed a copy of yours to Douglas Bader of 28 May 1945. Having re-read your fascinating account, and looked at Douglas Bader's story of that day, I wonder if I may be so bold as to ask you some other questions relating to those events?
>
> If you will, please forgive my temerity. However, there are published accounts of Douglas Bader's demise which proffer the view that he may well have been the victim of what journalists are now keen to call "friendly fire". This supposition is based upon the lack of any documentary evidence of any kills or claims by the Germans which can be made to match the loss of Bader, as well as the lack of any evidence which links his loss with a possible collision involving a Messerschmitt 109.
>
> Having re-read your account to Bader, I must say that there are striking similarities in your attack upon an Me 109 and what happened at exactly the same time, and in the same area, to Bader himself (i.e. singleton, cannon-fire severing almost all of the tail and the pilot finally baling out at around 6,000ft). Given that the Germans were, by this time, using the Me 109 F with their almost elliptical wingtips like the Spitfire then could a mistake of identification be made in the heat of combat? Under these circumstances, therefore, is it possible that your Me 109 could have been Bader's Spitfire? I wonder if that possibility has ever crossed your mind, or if it was a view that Bader himself ever expressed to you? With only seconds to distinguish between friend and foe, and in a situation of "kill or be killed", might an error of identification have been possible? Against the sun or a bright sky, under the stressed conditions of combat and with aeroplanes moving at an infinite number of angles in relation to each other, surely it must have been a possibility?
>
> From the viewpoint of an historian I seek only to examine, and record, all of the possibilities and I hope very much that you will not be offended by my questions to you. If the nature of my questions on this matter offend you then please accept my apologies, but it was only after months of deliberation that I decided to ask you these questions directly. Others, I am sure, are likely to raise the same questions and queries in the years and decades to come. It would be wonderful to get the unequivocal view of one who was there – your good self!

It had been a difficult and tortuously agonising letter to write and there was no way to soften the direct nature of questioning. However, the author was aware that there were others (a number of journalists amongst them) who had an inkling of this story and those who had already begun to put the disjointed pieces of the puzzle together. One day, inevitably, the story of possible friendly fire would come out with a link to Buck Casson. Better by far, surely, that the key player be asked for his view whilst he was still with us? The response, when it came, was not from Casson himself but from a third party acting in the interests of the Casson family.

Sadly, and without the knowledge of the author, Buck Casson had been suffering from a serious and debilitating illness at the time of writing to him. The response, on behalf of his wife, stated that this was obviously a potentially distressing matter for the Casson family to deal with and that Mrs Casson was, understandably, at a loss to know how to do so. The letter went on to reveal that this subject had already been researched and aired by another author, a trained detective, who had already published an account of the action which had not directly attributed friendly fire as the cause of Bader's loss. Further, the third party went on to state that apparently no new or compelling facts (other than those already published by the aforementioned detective) had come to light, and that in his view this was an important ingredient that was missing. In fact, the detective's report sparked further intrigue.

In the published material Buck Casson's action on 9 August 1941 was related and this followed, *almost* verbatim, the copy of the letter from Casson to Bader of 28 May 1945 which was already in this author's hands. There was, however, a vitally important omission – *any* reference to it having been a letter to Bader was left out, and the reader was given the impression that this was a more recent first-person account of the episode. Crucially, the *whole* paragraph where Casson describes having shot the tail off a Messerschmitt 109, and then having watched the pilot struggle to bale out before finally doing so at 6,000ft, had been edited out completely. No mention was made elsewhere in the published work of such an episode ever having taken place.

It was impossible to ignore the very clear discrepancies emerging between the primary source document (Casson's letter to Bader) and a subsequently published version of this account. It was important to question the matter further and to ask: why had a specific and obviously highly relevant portion of the account been "air brushed" out? However, given the impasse following the firm rebuff from the Casson family representative, it was difficult to continue the investigation much further. For the time being, at least, the mystery remained and it seemed impossible to progress. One day, though, someone surely would.

Unfortunately, Squadron Leader L H Casson passed away on 8 October 2003 at his Sheffield home and it was almost immediately afterwards that the well respected freelance journalist John Crossland contacted the author. Coincidentally, John had been educated at Casson's old school, Birkdale, and had also taken a keen interest in the Bader story. It emerged that he too was aware of that curious letter of 28 May 1945 and had begun to speculate as to what might have happened. Very shortly, it seemed, the story would probably be out there in the wider world. It was easy to imagine how the newspapers might treat such a scoop if they got it, and the more irresponsible elements of the media might not let the facts get in the way of a good story. At John Crossland's encouragement, and with the plethora of related facts now in the author's archive, the business of finally putting the account into the public domain was embarked upon.

It was a decision that would stir more than a little controversy, but it was one taken to pre-empt any half-baked and insensitive treatment of the story by the more sensational elements of the news industry. Not least of all, if the theory of friendly fire was to be further advanced, then there was a desire to do so in a sympathetic way and one that did not set out on a witch-hunt of Buck Casson, but rather to protect his name and reputation. The question remained, however; who would be prepared to "publish and be damned"?

Fortunately, Winston Ramsey, editor of World War Two history magazine *After the Battle* had both the courage and foresight to agree that the story must be told once he had reviewed all of the author's factual evidence. Consequently, he commissioned "Who Downed Douglas Bader?" for issue No 125 of the magazine, scheduled for publication during 2004. This gave time for further field work, and to assemble and examine any more facts that could be gleaned from all available sources. Accordingly, an opportunity to search again for the wreck of Bader's Spitfire now presented itself as part of the research for *After The Battle* and to re-examine what was known about crashes in the likely vicinity where Bader was brought down.

During a visit to the St Omer region in March 2004 the author covered again some of the ground taken in by the Malvern Spitfire Team in 1996 and, in addition, an effort was made to identify *all* known wartime air crashes in the immediate vicinity of the supposed Bader parachute landing site. In total, there were seven sites that might perhaps be considered; a reported Spitfire near La Vallée Ferme, Racquinghem, another Spitfire beside the road at Blaringhem, the supposed Spitfire at Mont Dupil, the German aircraft between Aire-sur-la-Lys and Boeseghem, an unidentified British aeroplane near Wittes, a Messerschmitt 109 at Wittes and another Spitfire north of Boeseghem – the latter already excavated in 1996 by the Malvern team.

Of the others, the remaining German aircraft had yet to be identified as positively associated with Circus 68 and the British aeroplane at Wittes was quickly identified as a 107 Squadron Blenheim (R3823) lost on 30 June 1940. The Messerschmitt 109 incident at Wittes was also easily identifiable and found to be the Me 109 F flown by Hauptmann Wilhelm Balthasar, Kommodore of JG 2, that had crashed into Ferme Goset at Wittes on 3 July 1941, killing its pilot. That left three known or suspected Spitfire crash locations worthy of further investigation as potentially being the site where Bader's aeroplane had impacted.

Initially, the most promising seemed to be the Mont Dupil site and it was to this location that Dubreu and Goblet now pointed. However, caution needed to be exercised in relation to the veracity of this assertion. After all, it had been Dubreu and Goblet who had originally, and so very emphatically, pointed to the Spitfire crash site north of Boeseghem which had led to the excavation of that site in 1996. When the wreckage there proved not to be Bader's aeroplane the two Frenchmen changed their minds and concluded that the crash at Mont Dupil must be the one after all. Yet neither had visited that particular crash site despite information that the aeroplane was in pieces across quite a big area of farmland which might indeed point to a break-up consequent upon the loss of a tail unit.

What made the possibility seem even more feasible in 2004, though, was the discovery that an artificial leg had been found in a field just a few hundred metres away from Mont Dupil. If that were the case, then this location certainly had promise and the crash site was accordingly scoured by detectors in March 2004. Not a shred of aircraft wreckage could be found, although a couple of *fired* .303 English bullet cases were discovered, both of them dated 1943.

Despite the initial excitement caused by these finds they could immediately be dismissed as unrelated to an aircraft crash site; all British .303 cartridge cases were ejected from fighter aircraft when fired and thus *spent* cases like these would not be present in a crashed aeroplane. Most likely they had fallen there from some later aerial combat, or perhaps they were even dropped by Allied ground troops during 1944. Monsieur Duhamel, however, the owner of Mont Dupil, recalled the crash that had happened there and described sections of what he thought to be fuselage laying in his father's paddock with some wreckage either in, or alongside, a solitary pear tree. In 2004 though (as in 1996) not a trace or scrap of aircraft debris could be found. M. Duhamel did, however, produce one other relevant piece of information.

Flt Sgt Donald Bostock of 122 Squadron who baled out of Spitfire MA764 near Blaringhem on 25 November 1943 and with his wife Alma on their wedding day.

In 1943 his father had hidden an RAF fighter pilot under sacks of potatoes in his cellar after he had baled out of a Spitfire. That pilot had been in contact with the Duhamel family during the post-war years. His name was Flight Sergeant Donald Bostock. Clearly, Bostock's aeroplane had crashed nearby but M.Duhamel was adamant it was not the one that had crashed in the Mont Dupil paddock. As he rightly pointed out, to have hidden an allied airman from the Germans was risky enough but to have hidden one from the Germans just a few steps from the aeroplane crash site was unthinkable. Furthermore, Duhamel was sure that the episode with the hidden fugitive pilot was much later than the actual Mont Dupil crash.

With the name of Donald Bostock to work with, the rest of that part of the puzzle was easy. Flight Sergeant Donald Bostock had been shot down on 25 November 1943, flying a Spitfire with 122 Squadron. Records relating to a subsequent MI9 interrogation of Bostock proved that he had indeed baled out about five miles north of Aire-sur-la-Lys, had been hidden under sacks of potatoes in a farmer's cellar and finally made it back to the United Kingdom via Gibraltar, eventually arriving home on 17 January 1944. With the nearest crash site to Mont Dupil (apart from the crash at the farm itself) being about two kilometres to the north-west at La Vallée Ferme, Racquinghem, it looked highly likely that this crash could be identified as Bostock's aeroplane and Bader could be eliminated from that location. The landowner, Madame Cappe, recalled the crash and said that it had happened six months before the death of her sister in a 1944 Allied bombing raid. This tied very neatly with the known Bostock crash date, but could not be considered conclusive given the question mark that surely had to be hung over the reliability of any such long-term eyewitness testimony. Apart from the German fighter, there only remained one further Spitfire crash that could be traced in the locality. This was on the edge of the road, just outside Blaringhem. Could this, perhaps, be Bader's crash site?

In this process of elimination, it was obviously necessary to examine a number of reports of other Spitfire losses in the area. One in particular attracted the author's attention and seemed to fit the general locality. On 8 June 1942 Sergeant J E Misseldine of 611 Squadron was shot down on a figher sweep over the St Omer area and baled out to land at Steenbecque. (Like Bostock, he hid and evaded – finally making it back to the UK on 8 September 1942.) The village of Steenbecque is just a few kilometres away from the roadside crash near Blaringhem and although not conclusive, it was a possible match. In the final analysis, however, only the recovery of parts from each of the known Spitfire crash sites *might* provide the answer conclusively. For now, the best guess was that the Bader crash site was at Mont Dupil. As for the German crash site near Aire-sur-la-Lys on the Route d'Hazebrouck, this was excavated on 15 June 2004 and as we saw in chapter seven proof had been found to link it to Circus 68. No other known possibilities for the crash site of Douglas Bader's Spitfire seemed to exist.

Sgt John "Jack" Misseldine of 611 Squadron.

For the time being, therefore, any physical quest for the last resting place of Douglas Bader's W3185, "Lord Lloyd", was put to bed and, later in 2004, the author's article appeared in *After The Battle* magazine suggesting for the first time that Bader may have fallen victim to friendly fire from Flight Lieutenant Buck Casson. It was a controversial revelation and, inevitably, resulted in a good deal of debate and angst, along with many claims of revisionism, sensationalism and disrespect for both Bader and Casson.

None of these claims were justified. It was, instead, simply a matter of genuinely trying to get to the truth and to present a fair and balanced view of all the evidence currently available. Perhaps it was inevitable, though, that the news media, from whom it had been intended to protect the name and reputation of Buck Casson, would now show an interest. Within a short time of the article appearing, the *Mail on Sunday* had taken a keen interest and ran an edited version of the article in its review supplement of 15 August 2004. The banner headline screamed: "Revealed: The Man Who Shot Down Douglas Bader (...and it wasn't a German)". With headlines like that, it was hard to see how the piece could save Casson from being publicly and unsympathetically labelled as "the man who got Bader" or to present the submissions in any kind of a reasoned and scholarly way.

Thankfully, the article followed more or less the exact text of the *After The Battle* piece. Only the headlines, across a four-page spread, lowered the tone of the reportage itself and gave some credence to accusations of sensationalising the story. "Even the Germans Lied to Protect Him" was another of the headlines dreamt up by the sub-editors. For now, though, the matter rested. The furore died down, Schlager's crash site had been identified and an educated best-guess – based on some reasonable circumstantial clues – had been made of the likely crash site of Bader's Spitfire. That said, whilst media interest in the story waned it had now captured the attention of a London-based television production company who specialised in making historical documentaries.

Amongst other programmes, Wildfire TV were the makers of the *Time Team* series and had long been interested in finding a suitable aviation archaeology subject. The Bader story, they felt, was an ideal candidate and they had already (and fortuitously as it turned out!) taken film footage of the Schlager "dig" as part of their development work for a proposed aviation archaeology documentary. The appearance of the *Mail on Sunday* feature strengthened the appeal for both programme makers and broadcasters alike, and, in due course, a two-hour documentary was commissioned by Channel 4 Television, with Wildfire TV engaging the author and the research material, which forms the basis of this book, to lead the documentary quest. The objective was to examine the friendly fire possibility and to take the viewer on a journey of investigation and discovery which would be based, largely, around a much more in-depth investigation of the various crash sites and the circumstances appertaining to each one. The hope was that new information or evidence might yet be forthcoming. The Casson "friendly fire" theory was still only a theory. But if we could find Bader's aircraft, we could quite possibly turn that theory into fact.

Chapter Thirteen

Continuing the Quest: The Television Documentary

During the late autumn of 2005 filming work commenced in the Pas de Calais region around St Omer and brought together, for a week of intense activity, a team of researchers and experts to search out the facts and, hopefully, tangible relics of the Bader episode. Assembled together in the author's team were a party of aviation archaeologists, along with Spitfire expert Peter Arnold and retired air accident investigator, Bernie Forward. Together, it was hoped the team might unlock more of the mystery and perhaps uncover the remains of Bader's Spitfire.

With such flimsy evidence to go on, it was all a bit of a long shot but the definite lead already provided by the identification of Schlager's aeroplane did at least provide a high degree of confidence that we had the right geographical area. If it were at all possible to find any Spitfire parts at Mont Dupil then it might just be feasible to link these to W3185 or, at the very least, maybe to a Spitfire Mk VA. Again, a long shot. But possible. As for the other Spitfire crashes identified, the intention was to rule them out or rule them in by pin-pointing the exact sites and then excavating them on camera. Spitfire historian Peter Arnold was on hand to help identify the recovered remains, the exact mark of Spitfire and maybe to aid in the physical identification of the serial numbers that would hopefully be recovered.

The crash site of Albert Schlager's Messerschmitt 109 was also on the list for re-excavation given that the earlier operation at the site had failed to recover the more substantial parts of the airframe. With knowledge gained at the first "dig" as to the precise depth and attitude of the wreckage there certainly remained a very good chance that, with the employment of more appropriate machinery, the remainder of the aircraft could be reached and recovered. This would enable air accident investigator Bernie Forward to examine the wreckage for both combat damage and any sign of mid-air collision. Vitally, if a collision had occurred then paint transference from that collision, or possibly even embedded Spitfire components, might just be found.

Far fetched though this may seem, evidence of mid-air collision has more than once been found in post-war aircraft recoveries – a good example being the discovery of belted rounds of British .303 bullets impacted deeply into a wing part of a Dornier 17 Z that had been downed over Kent on 7 September 1940 following a mid-air collision with a Spitfire – the bullets being embedded there when the Spitfire's wing sliced into the Dornier. If anyone was likely to find forensic evidence of such a collision then it was Forward.

His credentials were impeccable; a former service pilot, test pilot and then officer

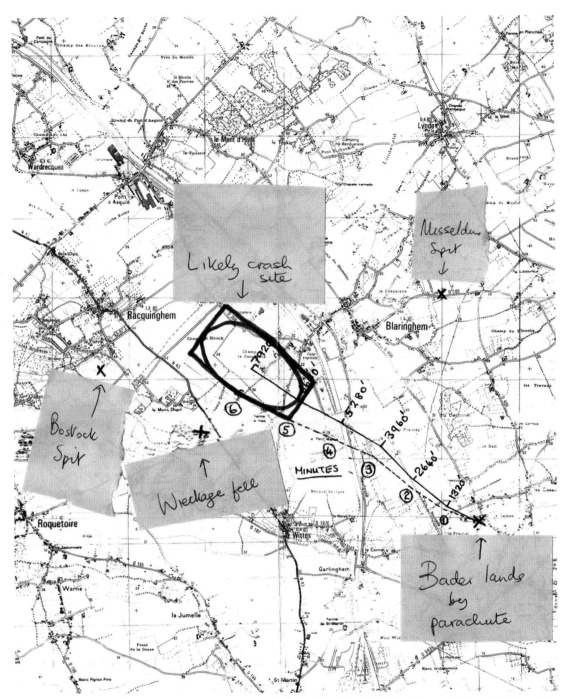

The handwritten annotations on the map read:

- Likely crash site ↓
- Misselden Spit ↓
- Bostock Spit ↑
- Wreckage fell ↑
- MINUTES
- Bader lands by parachute ↑

The original map used during the televised search for Bader's Spitfire in 2005 with annotations. Significantly, this map has the track of Bader's parachute descent marked on it by senior meteorological office forecaster Jim Allen. Tracking back from the parachute landing site the unbroken line gives the estimated track over land, with duration in minutes marked from one to six – the point at which he leaves the Spitfire at around 8,000ft. Altitudes are then shown against the relevant time in the descent. The dotted line gives the boundary of any likely margin of error. The large oval within a square is Bernie Forward's calculated hot zone. It will be seen by comparing this map with the photograph (page 95) that Bader's calculated exit point was close to Mont Dupil and more or less directly above the spot where wing wreckage and the artificial leg were found.

A panoramic view of the area around Blaringhem in the Pas de Calais where Bader and his Spitfire fell on 9 August 1941. (1) Mont Dupil Farm where wreckage from Spitfire W3185 fell and where, later, Flt Sgt Donald Bostock was hidden from the Germans in the cellar. (2) The approximate area where the Duhamel family saw the wreckage. (3) The other side of the N43 road where wing wreckage and Bader's detached artificial leg were found. (4) Where Bader landed by parachute. *(Winston Ramsey)*

commanding the Bomber & Maritime Test Squadron, Aircraft & Armament Experimental Establishment, Boscombe Down. Latterly, and upon retirement from the service, he had become an air accident investigator and had taken a lead role in the Lockerbie Boeing 747 disaster investigations. All the same, and notwithstanding his qualifications, we were dealing with some pretty vague sixty-year-old evidence in this particular instance. Bernie's clues were usually rather more fresh than that!

The initial area of interest was the farm at Mont Dupil, as this still remained the team's first choice to be the crash site of W3185. Interestingly, it was located just a few hundred metres to the west of the site where the articial leg had been found on farmland alongside the N43 road. As intimated in chapter ten, it also happened to be just a few hundred metres from the spot on the map that marked Jim Allen's calculated exit point for Bader from his Spitfire. Unaware of the Mont Dupil location, Bernie Forward used Allen's calculations to estimate what he called a "hot zone" and into which he felt Bader's Spitfire may have fallen. Incredibly, the western periphery of that zone just about skirted Mont Dupil. If nothing else then it was a truly amazing coincidence. It also gave a degree of scientific credibility for the Mont Dupil site to be the correct target.

Filming underway at Mont Dupil in the meadow where wreckage of Bader's Spitfire is believed to have fallen. *(P Arnold)*

Using the information from Monsieur Duhamel, and now the calculations of Jim Allen and Bernie Forward, searches for physical evidence of a crash site at both Mont Dupil and within Bernie Forward's hot zone were initiated and acted out in front of the cameras. In the case of the hot zone, many acres of farmland around Champs de la Carpenterie and Champs du Houck were covered by a metal detecting team comprising Peter Dimond, Richard Barnstable, Tim Davies, Simon Parry, Vince Megicks, Paul Cole and Phillipa Wheeler. This team was led by Gareth Jones. Hundreds of acres were duly tramped and detected in miserably cold conditions but the fields were relatively clean of any metal detritus and only a small handful of dropped coins, shrapnel and agricultural hardware were found for such a vast area. The area was totally clean of any identifiable aircraft debris. There was no local knowledge whatsoever of any aircraft crash having occurred within Bernie's hot zone, but no stone was left unturned – almost quite literally!

Determined to either find or rule out the possibility of there being any living eyewitnesses of the Bader incident, a dragnet was then trawled across all the local villages and appeals placed in the regional press. Letters were sent to every household and every registered address within a good few kilometres of Mont Dupil. Doors were knocked on, various mayors canvassed for information and all the local bars and cafés scoured for those with any bit of knowledge – however small. In all, it was an extensive enquiry operation that would have been a credit to any police force – but it was all to no avail. Then, one witness

The author (right) confers with team colleagues at Mont Dupil during filming by Wildfire TV in the autumn of 2005. L to R: Paul Cole, Peter Dimond and Bernie Forward (centre) the retired air accident inspector. *(P Arnold)*

came forward who remembered a "Spitfire being hit by flak and falling out of the sky in pieces somewhere between Aire and Blaringhem". Since this account could not be tied into any other "known" Spitfire loss in the immediate vicinity, this observation was certainly very interesting. Had he seen the disintegration of Bader's Spitfire?

To the Frenchman, the only plausible explanation for the mid-air disintegration of a Spitfire might well have been a flak hit. If there were any other living witnesses to events at Mont Dupil, though, they could not be found. Going with the information available it was clearly time to turn again to the favoured location at Mont Dupil farm where M Duhamel had indicated the position where he had recalled seeing wreckage. As an eleven-year-old boy, the debris in his

Left: Assembled onto a wooden framework of a Spitfire fuselage, this was the recovered wreckage of Donald Bostock's Spitfire, MA764, after it had been returned to the UK, cleaned, and prepared for filming. *(P Arnold)*

Right: Another view of the Bostock wreckage, showing the cockpit. *(P Arnold)*

Left: A view showing the fuselage roundel from MA764. Considering its age, location and the nature of the crash the wreckage was remarkably well preserved. *(P Arnold)*

Above: P7973 is today preserved at the Australian War Memorial in Canberra. A surviving veteran of Circus 68, albeit with a sadly questionable record in respect of its participation that day.
(P Arnold)

Top right: This poster for Reach for the Sky was a trade advertisement in a 1956 edition of *Kinematographic Weekly*.

Right: Incredibly, P8332 is yet another surviving Spitfire from Circus 68. Today it is preserved in the Canadian War Museum at Ottawa although the sharp-eyed will notice that the original propeller assembly has been replaced with non-Spitfire blades that have squared-off tips. It is truly amazing that two genuine Spitfires that took part in Circus 68 with Bader are still in existence.
(P Arnold)

Digging deep for clues. Here, the author's team excavate the crash site of the Widdebrouck Messerschmitt 109 in the summer of 2004. At over twenty-five feet the tailwheel emerged along with a small data tag identifying the aircraft as a victim of Circus 68 operations – the Messerschmitt 109 F flown by Uffz Albert Schlager. In this view the deeply buried wreckage had not yet been reached!

father's back meadow just off the Rue Pont du Henaux had left an indelible impression on his memory. So here, at Mont Dupil, a much more scientific search was conducted.

Initially, the field was measured and surveyed and a scale plan drawn up of what is an almost uniformly rectangular pasture. On the plan, a grid was constructed giving a total of ninety numbered plots, each of ten metres square, and each

Although no metal detector readings were picked up at the believed site where the Bader wreckage fell, excavations were carried out there – just in case! Patrick Fleming, the film's director, stands rear right. *(P Arnold)*

one was scanned by the metal detecting team – each team member having his allocated and grid-patterned search area. Once a square had been searched it was either eliminated or any positive reading marked on the ground and the chart and the plot then marked off as checked before moving on to the next square. Again, as with Bernie Forward's tentative hot zone, the field was remarkably clean. Of all ninety plots examined, only fourteen showed up any metal detector readings at all and these fourteen squares were then scanned using a Forster deep-seeking bomb locator.

None of the fourteen revealed any deeply buried items and all of the metallic objects already located by detectors in each of the "dirty" squares were duly excavated. Again, not a shred of aircraft-related metalwork was found. Instead, a plethora of bottle tops, domestic rubbish, tin cans, dropped coins, horse shoes and general agricultural debris was uncovered. Much of the domestic rubbish was found in the squares with close proximity to the hedge bordering an adjacent domestic dwelling – all of these being items that had been carelessly tossed into the field from the garden of that house.

Of the squares covering the precise area indicated by M Duhamel, none had revealed metal of any kind. Just to be sure, the entire field was scanned again by the deep-seeking Forster with special attention being paid to the spot indicated by Duhamel, which was then excavated by mechanical excavator as a final reassurance. The results were negative, as was an exhaustive search of wartime and post-war aerial photographs of Mont Dupil that were painstakingly examined by team member Simon Parry, with every shadow and blemish scrutinised on the photos, enhanced on a lap-top computer and examined on the ground. Again, nothing.

The whole team was deflated. If Bader's Spitfire had impacted here then not a single shred of it remained to be found. In the view of the investigating team it was highy unusual not to find a single trace of forensic evidence from such an impact if one had indeed occurred here. Investigations at Mont Dupil had drawn a blank once more and the experienced team were now entirely satisfied that nothing at all was to be found at the reported crash site given the professional and meticulous thoroughness with which the search had been conducted. However, the absence of evidence did not necessarily mean nothing had happened here. Meanwhile, the other potential Bader crash site beside the road at Blaringhem was under investigation too.

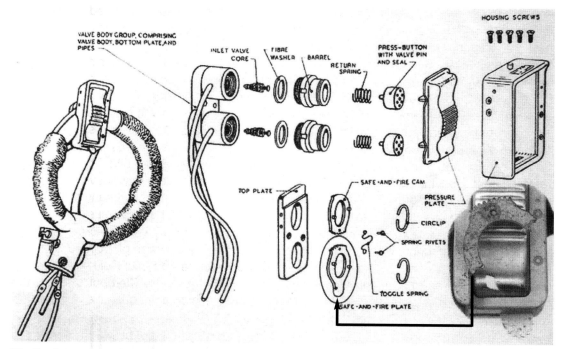

The tiny internal component from the control column of "Jack" Misseldine's Spitfire. The recovered component is shown (bottom right) superimposed over the gun button of the same type of control column fitted to Misseldine's Spitfire and is also shown in relation to the technical drawing of the control column grip from an air ministry publication. *(P Arnold)*

Here, Monsieur Goblet was completely adamant about the position of the crash aftermath he had witnessed as a young boy. He was certain, too, that this was not Bader's aeroplane, but he was also equally sure about the precise crash location. As it turned out, Georges was right. Almost exactly where he had indicated, fragments of Spitfire wreckage were found on the surface of the field and local plant hire contractor, André Clerbout, was employed to use a mechanical excavator to dig out any buried wreckage for the cameras. Peter Arnold was on hand, although there was unfortunately very little at this site for him to identify. What remained was sparse, and comprised mainly of splintered sections of wooden Rotol propeller blade, shattered glass from an armoured windscreen and tiny fragments of engine and airframe.

In itself, the discovery of wooden propeller parts indicated this was probably not Bader's machine as photographic evidence exists to show that W3185 had an alloy de Havilland airscrew. There was, however, one small but very important find that enabled Peter Arnold to declare that this was most definitely *not* the crash site of W3185. Amongst the one or two finds in the boxes of recovered artefacts was a small alloy gear, an otherwise insignificant object but identifiable in this instance as the safety catch from the gun button on a Spitfire control column. In this particular case it was from a cannon-armed Spitfire, therefore ruling out a machine-gun equipped Mk VA and thus ruling out Bader's aeroplane. If it were needed, a further indication that this was a later Spitfire came with the discovery of the brass bezel of the instrument panel clock of a type not yet in use during 1941. So, only one more site to go!

The site at La Vallée Ferme, Racquinghem, was still considered by the team to most likely have been the aeroplane abandoned by Flight Sergeant Donald Bostock in November 1943

– although there was so far no absolute proof. Even the time-line established by Madame Cappe through the death of her late sister could not be absolutely certain. Not only that, but its close proximity to Mont Dupil and both Jim Allen's exit point and Bernie Forward's hot zone could not be ignored. With nothing at all found at Mont Dupil, and nothing conclusive by the road at Blaringhem, team member Tim Davies argued vociferously for the excavation of the Racquinghem site in the face of an initially wavering stance by producer Simon Raikes and director Patrick Fleming as to whether or not to proceed with this dig.

Simon, not unreasonably, took the view that Mme Cappe's apparently firm establishment of a date effectively ruled out this location. But what if Madame Cappe was wrong? After all, Goblet and Debreu had already been mistaken over the Archer/Bader site. The team were therefore not convinced by Simon's argument, and contended that leaving this site unchecked could turn into a disaster (especially for the TV production company) if any other party excavated there after the team had left and found it to have been Bader's Spitfire after all. Over a good many beers in the Hotel Ibis, St Omer, the Wildfire crew and the investigation team concurred with Tim Davies. Ultimately, the site was pinpointed by Vince Megicks after a long search and excavated in an operation led by Paul Cole – once again utilising the services of avuncular local plant hire contractor, André Clerbout. At first, the signs looked encouraging and there were certainly considerable quantities of aircraft wreckage buried here. The question was – who was the pilot?

Just a short way into the recovery operation, substantial wreckage was being unearthed, entombed deeply in the soft clay which, when disturbed, spilt out gallon upon gallon of high octane aviation spirit that had been trapped there since the crash. Quite early on in the operation it also became apparent that absolutely none of the tail section or fuselage aft of the radio mast was present with the buried wreckage. This was an interesting discovery – the potential significance of which was not lost on film director Patrick Fleming or on dig leader Paul Cole. Amongst the wreckage then

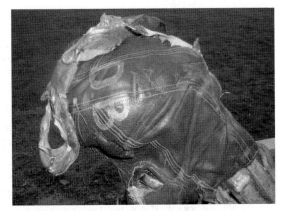

A huge surprise for the recovery team was this discarded flying helmet and pair of goggles found in the cockpit and marked with the letters DB. *(P Dimond)*

brought to the surface was a wrapped-up mass of aluminium alloy which proved to have once been the cockpit of a Spitfire. Out of it, and onto the wet soil, fell a wrapped up ball of muddy leather – quickly and easily identifiable as an RAF flying helmet.*

Given the nature of the quest which had prompted this particular recovery, the team were amazed to discover that it was a B type helmet of the zip-eared pattern that had been in use during 1941. If this *had* been the November 1943 crash, it would surely have more likely been a C type helmet with its rubber earphone cups, then in almost exclusive use by RAF aircrew, having superceded the earlier B type helmet. Further examination of the helmet gave the recovery team yet another start, revealing two large initials painted onto its crown in bold white letters: DB.

---

*Pilots, as standard practice, generally removed their flying headgear prior to any bale out in order to minimise the risk of entanglement in radio telephone leads or oxygen tubes – and thus the discovery of such items in wrecked aircraft does not necessarily point to any other perhaps more macabre explanation.

It did not take long to register with the team, though, that the other pilot-candidate for this Spitfire, Donald Bostock, shared the same initials as Bader. Despite the initial excitement it soon became apparent, too, that this was a much later Mk IX Spitfire fitted with 20mm cannons and wearing a post-1941 camouflage and markings scheme. The final proof, however, came with the discovery in the cockpit and on the firewall of data plates which confirmed the history. Spitfire historian Peter Arnold explains:

> The Spitfire airframe construction numbering system is complex, and if Vickers Supermarine had known they were eventually going to build over 22,000 examples in various scattered locations instead of the original three hundred-odd then I am sure the system would have been different. The main fuselage monocoque carries a small data plate on the right-hand side of the cockpit. The Frame 5 firewall, a separate sub assembly which is riveted and bolted to the main fuselage, also carries a data plate but with a different number. Neither of these two data plates make any reference to the RAF airframe serial number and there is no central document surviving – if one ever existed – that cross refers these construction numbers with the RAF serials.

Over a substantial number of years, by inspection, a database has been built up of these data plate numbers on all the known extant Spitfires worldwide. It is therefore possible to make a judgement on "new find" construction plates to approximate where they were built in the Spitfire production schedule and, therefore, the RAF serial number related to that particular data plate. In the case of the Spitfire which Donald Bostock was known to have abandoned, the recovered wreckage – which was believed to be the remains of MA764 – was found to contain both the cockpit and data plates. The cockpit plate read CBAF IX 401. This indicates it was the 401st Mk IX Spitfire built at the Castle Bromwich Aeroplane Factory. The firewall plate reads CBAF 5423.

This tag on the cockpit wreckage read CBAF IX 401, which helped Spitfire historian Peter Arnold positively to identify the wreckage as that of MA764. The importance of even tiny bits of recovered evidence is highlighted here, as is the need to interpret skilfully such finds. *(P Arnold)*

The RAF serial numbers and data plate numbers do not run sequentially, and although this varies they are *usually* within + / – 20 when considering, say, a couple of hundred Spitfires. An existing Mk IX Spitfire, MH350, is a museum example in Norway and has the cockpit plate number CBAF IX 490. There were eighty-five Spitfires built alpha-numerically between MA764 and MH350 and there is a construction number variance of (490-401) 89. Irrespective of the DB flying helmet and other circumstantial evidence linking this machine to Don Bostock's MA764 I am of the view that to be within just four digits would be proof beyond doubt that MA764 had been located.

Team members Paul Cole (left) and Peter Dimond with the 20mm cannon excavated from the Spitfire wreckage at Racquinghem. This gave clear proof that this wreck was not Bader's W3185 which was only equipped with .303 Browning machine guns.

By a process of elimination, therefore, the Spitfire by the road at Blaringhem could now quite confidently be identified as BM303, the Spitfire VB abandoned by Jack Misseldine on 8 June 1942. The filmed discovery of Bostock's wreck, though, without any of its tail section present and the subsequent unearthing of a correct pattern flying helmet for 1941 (and with "DB" marked on it!) was surely a dream come true for the director of the documentary, Patrick Fleming, in his quest for an element of mystery and suspense. The declaration, though, that this was most certainly Bostock's Spitfire brought Mont Dupil very firmly back into the frame as the Bader crash site. Or did it?

The activities around St Omer in November 2005 excited local press and resulted in a good deal of coverage of the discoveries of the film crew and the investigation team. In turn, this attracted public attention and, in particular, a M René Dewasmes of Aire-sur-la-Lys who came forward to tell the team that he knew of another crash site, he believed of a Spitfire, near the village of Wittes which is located just a few kilometres south-south-east of Mont Dupil. Dewasmes, who had witnessed the crash as a boy was able to point out the spot at Ferme de St Martin where he had seen the burning wreckage. A search revealed no trace of aircraft-related debris but established that hedge boundaries to the surrounding fields had since been moved following post-war construction of a gravel quarry, now disused, which had eventually become a lake.

In all likelihood, the impact point was now encroached on by that lake and, in any event, no evidence – circumstantial or otherwise – existed to identify this crash as: (a) British, (b) Bader's Spitfire, or (C) linked in *any* way to Circus 68. It was entirely likely that what Dewasmes was remembering was the partial wreckage of Hauptmann Balthasar's Messerschmitt 109 of JG 2, known to have fallen in pieces over the St Martin/Wittes area on 3 July 1941. The completed documentary, however, suggested that the crash site near the lake at St Martin could well be where Bader's Spitfire fell. However, a more rigorous re-examination of the known losses in the area, post-filming, now points to the Balthasar Me 109 connection, with the Mont Dupil location thereby being reinstated as favourite for the Bader crash site.

Save for some tidying-up on the filming front, and the filling in of a few other gaps in the documentary, the programme was just about in the can. "A wrap" in film-speak. But was it "a wrap" for the investigators? Unfortunately, the re-excavation of Albert Schlager's Messerschmitt 109 for further filming and investigation had proved impossible as the landowner was now asking too high a price of Wildfire TV for a facility fee which would allow them to proceed. Luckily, Wildfire already had footage from the earlier excavation at the site and evidence was also to hand as to the identity of both the aeroplane and its pilot. Not only that, but it had been established that the crash happened with the tail unit intact – an all important detail. The re-excavation of this site, therefore, was not considered crucial by the film makers.

Two remaining aspects of the documentary had yet to be filmed. First, the Battle HQ (Gefechtsstand) of Galland near his JG 26 base at Audembert was covered – and the underground bunker constructed in the garden of Le Colombier, the farmhouse requisitioned by the Luftwaffe and dubbed by the locals as "Maison Galland". It was here that Bader had been brought for the historic meeting with members of Galland's wing and to be entertained for tea. Here, too, was the location – almost unchanged – where Bader was photographed with Galland and the entourage of his officers and staff. Just along the road was the aerodrome where Bader was photographed sitting in a Messerschmitt 109 cockpit. The television crew's filming at "Maison Galland" added some further interest and colour to the overall story, and it was certainly incredible to be able to pinpoint the exact place where this significant meeting had occurred.

Later, another filming session was set up with noted aviation historians Chris Shores and Don Caldwell (both Grub Street authors) and the author, for an over-view of events on 9 August 1941. It was an exercise that would set out, televisually, the sequence of events that day, squadron by squadron, and enabled debate on the day's action by the three participating authors. At the end of this shoot, Don Caldwell (the Texas-based JG 26 historian) declared his view that none of the pilots from JG 26 "claimed" Bader and that he was "very likely" to have been the victim of friendly fire. Ultimately, this would indeed be the overall conclusion of the finished documentary. But we still hadn't found his 'plane

Eventually, and to generally positive reviews by newspaper TV critics, the two-hour documentary "Who Downed Douglas Bader?" was first screened on Channel 4 in the United Kingdom on bank holiday Monday, 28 August 2006. To some, though, the suggestion of friendly fire still seemed anathema.

CHAPTER FOURTEEN

FRIENDLY FIRE – THE PHENOMENON EXAMINED

The term "friendly fire" is, perhaps, something of a misnomer both in the context of this book specifically, and within the usage of the English language generally. It is, however, terminology that is widely understood by the public at large and this is due, at least in part, to widespread media coverage of unfortunate episodes during the first and second Gulf wars. It is a misnomer in the context of this book, though, because it is in reality an exclusively modern American military term.

In British military terms "blue on blue" would be more accurate – this being a descriptive deriving from Cold War usage of blue map markers for Allied, NATO or "friendly" forces and orange ones for the enemy. More accurately, the Oxford English dictionary has another word for it; fratricide, defined as the accidental killing of one's own forces during time of war, however this cannot be accurately applied to this case since no fatality actually occurred.

As World War Two terminology, though, neither the expression friendly fire or blue on blue is strictly accurate even though the actual phenomenon is as old as warfare itself. To be specific, non-hostile fire can be placed into three distinct categories; accidental mis-identification, deliberate mis-identification ("fragging" to the US Military in the Vietnam era) or mis-directed fire which hits friendly forces often through errors of positioning. As a distinction, though, it is important to clarify that friendly fire should be regarded as fire that is generally *intended* to do harm to the enemy and not an event arising through accidental firing. Contrary to what might seem to be the case through present-day newspaper and media reports it is far from being a new aspect of 20th or 21st Century warfare that somehow first manifested itself during the recent Gulf conflicts.

In 1412, for example, at the Battle of Towton during the Wars of The Roses, strong winds caused arrows to fall amongst friendly troops as well as among the ranks of the enemy. At Waterloo, Marshal Blucher's Prussian artillery fired mistakenly at their Allies, the British, and British artillery returned the fire resulting in considerable casualties on both sides. Throughout history, the list is almost endless and possibly the most infamous episode of friendly fire in the World War Two annals of the RAF was at the well recorded Battle of Barking Creek. Here, RAF Spitfires mistakenly engaged and shot down two Hurricanes resulting in the death of one pilot (Pilot Officer Hulton-Harrop of 56 Squadron) in an appalling blunder on 6 September 1939, thereby making Hulton-Harrop the RAF's first fighter pilot casualty of the war – and by the hand of his own service. These, it is important to realise, were far from isolated incidents and it is also essential to appreciate that if the loss of

Douglas Bader on 9 August 1941 were to be attributed to friendly fire then it would hardly be an extraordinary occurrence.

The history of the RAF in World War Two is liberally sprinkled with accounts of pilots mistaking friendly fighters for the enemy. On 5 September, 1940 for example, Pilot Officer Robin Rafter of 603 Squadron wrote of his experiences in combat that day, saying: "I very nearly shot a Spitfire down by mistake…." So, the evidence that it happened is certainly out there and these cases cannot all be put down to inexperience. Neither can the Battle of Barking Creek be attributed wholly to nervous jitters arising out of the uncertainty of the very early days of war.

Towards the war's end, on 26 May 1944 a squadron of Spitfires attacked Spitfires of 43 Squadron over Lake Bracciano, Italy, resulting in the downing of Flying Officer Cassels who became PoW. Later, on 11 November 1944, we have another instance where Spitfires, again of 43 Squadron, were "bounced" over Padua, Italy, this time by USAAF P-51s resulting in the death of Flight Lieutenant Cummings and severe damage to another Spitfire flown by Flight Lieutenant Creed. The P-51 pilots all believed they had attacked and shot down Messerschmitt 109s.

Back to 9 August 1941 though, and we have an official RAF report for that date stating *categorically* that Spitfires of 485 Squadron were attacked by six other Spitfires during Circus 68 itself. Thus it should not be any great surprise or controversial revelation that friendly fire was involved that day. The evidence is there for all to read at the national archives in Kew.

The Luftwaffe were also far from being immune from such episodes. On 30 September 1940 Group Captain Stanley Vincent, RAF, observed two Messerschmitt 109s engaged in mortal combat near Dorking. What he had seen was another Me 109 engaging that flown by Leutnant Herbert Schmidt of JG 27, who was ultimately shot down wounded and taken

Two photographs showing the severed tail plane of a Messerschmitt 109 E brought down over Surrey on 30 September 1940. The assembly has been blown clean away from the aircraft by a 20mm cannon shell that has entered through the elevator and then exploded inside the structure of the horizontal stabilizer with devastating effect. Only very few RAF fighter aircraft were cannon-equipped during 1940, and none of them were anywhere in the vicinity. It is therefore safe to conclude that the destruction of this Messerschmitt was the result of accurate shooting by a cannon-armed Me 109 – thus providing us with an excellent illustration of both friendly fire and the deadly power of explosive cannon shells. A twenty pence coin gives scale to the exit point of the 20mm shell through the leading edge of the elevator. *(Eddie Taylor)*

prisoner when a single 20mm cannon shell exploded and blew his starboard tail plane clean away. No RAF fighters with 20mm cannon were engaged in that combat, and so the fatal shot was definitely German. The evidence is there to see in the preserved tail plane, testimony both to the lethal effects of exploding 20mm cannon shells and to the not unusual occurrence of friendly fire. A Luftwaffe loss more closely tied in time to the events of Circus 68, though, is related in the operations record book of 603 Squadron for a sortie flown later in the evening of 9 August 1941. It is noted that what was thought to be a Messerschmitt 109 was seen going down in flames over France and, it was believed, had been mistakenly shot down by the enemy.

After the author's initial publication of the suggestion that Bader may have been a friendly fire victim, and the further investigation of that issue within the television documentary, a certain degree of criticism was levelled at those making such assertions. Some believed that such suggestions were "revisionist", and if Bader said he had been involved in a collision then he had. Equally, if an RAF fighter pilot had said he shot down a Messerschmitt 109 then he obviously had. It was also said that the memory of great fighter pilots like Buck Casson was being tarnished and that the record of the RAF's achievement, generally, was being besmirched.

The author strongly refutes all such suggestions, although putting forward uncomfortable facts like these is always bound to provoke some reaction. After all, one of the laws of the universe is that any action provokes a reaction! It is impossible, though, simply to ignore the reality of the facts and the evidence to hand. Equally, it is vitally important to look at all such information in a measured and balanced manner without letting sensationalism get in the way. As a fundamental point, then, let us accept that friendly fire is an unfortunate fact of war.

To put things into context for the RAF fighter pilot of the period, perhaps nobody could express it better than Wing Commander "Paddy" Barthropp when he described some of the difficulties faced by a young pilot who flew fighters into battle at that time:

> He had total control of a 400mph fighter and eight machine guns – with no radar, no auto-pilot and no electronics. At the touch of a button he could unleash thirteen pounds of shot in three seconds. He had a total of fourteen seconds of ammunition. He needed to be less than two hundred and fifty yards from the enemy to be effective. He and his foe could manoeuvre in three dimensions at varying speeds with an infinite number of angles relative to each other. His job was to solve the sighting equation without becoming a target himself.
>
> His aircraft carried ninety gallons of fuel between his chest and the engine. He often flew up to over 25,000ft with no cockpit heating or pressurisation. He endured up to six times the force of gravity with no "G" suit. He had about three seconds in which to identify his foe, and only slightly longer to abandon the aircraft if hit. Often, as in my case, he was only nineteen years old. He was considered too young and irresponsible to vote, but not too young to die.

Barthropp's words, from one who was there, give a gripping insight into what it meant to be a fighter pilot flying a Spitfire into combat. All the same, he doesn't mention the fear or the adrenalin-surged stress and absolute draining fatigue of it all. It is easy now, as armchair aviators, to read combat reports and other first hand accounts and not to appreciate fully elements like the cold, the overpowering noise of the Merlin engine, the incessant crackle of the headphones and the often unintelligible shouts from other pilots, the stress of being over enemy held territory, or over the sea, and listening and watching for any faltering signs

A camera-gun shot of a Spitfire caught by Gerhard Schoepfel of JG 26 on 27 June 1941. Compare this with the camera-gun image of a Messerschmitt 109 F caught by an allied pilot (right) and the similarities of both aircraft from astern, against a bright sky and in the high stress situation of combat and the difficulties faced by fighter pilots of both sides can be appreciated. *(via Dr Alfred Price)*

from the engine. Not only that, but the mental strain of holding formation, looking constantly for an unseen enemy and the sheer physical effort and exertion of flying, too. To those on the ground it must have seemed a glamorous job. To some extent it was but more often than not the reality was far from glamorous.

In Barthropp's account he talks of the problems of sighting and identification, and the time in which he had to do both. A question of "kill or be killed". If we factor in all of the other physical and physiological elements – which might also include blurred vision from the high "G" manoeuvring and the difficulty of seeing clearly and identifying a potential target against a bright sky or the sun – it is very easy indeed to see how these friendly fire events happened. We also need to look at the specific aircraft type against which the pilots on Circus 68 were pitched – the Messerschmitt 109 F.

The F model was a relative newcomer to the Luftwaffe stable and its shape was far more rounded than the earlier E model which RAF Fighter Command had faced in 1940. With its rounded wingtips, domed spinner cone and the deletion of tail plane bracing struts, the view from almost dead astern of a Messerschmitt 109 F is uncannily similar in some respects to that presented by a Spitfire from the same angle. Even during the Battle of Britain, when RAF pilots were fighting the Messerschmitt 109 E with its squared off nose cone, tail bracing struts and squared off wing tips some pilots, like Robin Rafter, were making split second errors of identification. Now, in 1941, it had become even more challenging for them.

If we suppose, then, that Flight Lieutenant Buck Casson was most likely responsible for inadvertently shooting down his wing leader that day it is important to look at this mishap in an objective fashion. First, Casson was a skilled, experienced, well respected and well liked

The first Messerschmitt 109 F to fall into British hands intact was that flown by Hptm Rolf Pingel the commander of I Gruppe JG 26 who crash-landed after combat at St Margaret's Bay, Kent, 10 July 1941. Pingel was taken PoW but his interrogation provided a useful insight into Luftwaffe thinking in relation to the daylight missions then being flown by the RAF over France, (see Appendix N). The Messerschmitt 109 F was repaired and test flown by the RAF, but lost in an accident at Fowlmere on 20 October 1941.

fighter pilot – but as with all the other pilots that day he suffered the stresses and demands which Barthropp so succinctly encapsulated into his commentary. No degree or suggestion of blame is being attached to Casson here – or to any of the pilots involved that day in what may well have been terrible accidents resulting from the fog, speed and confusion of war. Who is this author – or any other – to lay blame at the door of a pilot who found himself in such a situation? Of course, there were many pilots (Casson amongst them, probably) who never realised their mistake. Some did, of course, and their inevitable sense of guilt or remorse can only be imagined. Perhaps, in a few cases, there may have been degrees of negligence or gross carelessness and even misconduct. In even fewer cases there may well have been deliberate acts, although the author is certainly not suggesting any of these factors came into play over the downing of Douglas Bader.

To put things into overall context then, it is interesting to note that US Pentagon sources cite a figure of anywhere between two percent and twelve percent of all World War Two casualties as being the result of friendly fire incidents. From Vietnam, to Desert Storm and to the invasion of Afghanistan the figures stand at anywhere between fourteen percent to twenty-three percent. True, these are specifically US military statistics but there is absolutely no reason to suppose that the figures for other conflicts, other nationalities, or other forces are very much different. Any detailed examination of known mis-identification or mis-directed fire episodes within the RAF during the 1939-45 period shows a surprisingly high incidence of such cases. One of these cases then, and based on all the available evidence, involved the downing of Douglas Bader.

CHAPTER FIFTEEN

AERODYNAMICS AND SCIENCE

In order better to understand what happened to Spitfire W3185 and its pilot when brought down over France, it is necessary to look at some of the principles relating to the theory of flight, and, in particular, the functional significance of an aeroplane's tail surfaces. In order to do this we are accepting that Spitfire W3185 lost either all or significant parts of its tail section. Whether the cause was collision or gunfire is immaterial for the purposes of this exercise.

In flight there are four forces exerted on an airframe which affect the stability of an aircraft, namely: weight, thrust, lift and drag. These forces combine and result in making an aeroplane pitch nose down, although it is the addition of a tail plane at the rear of the aircraft which, in most circumstances, provides a download counteracting the natural tendency of the aircraft to dive. The elevators on the tail allow the download being exerted on the tail plane to be varied by the pilot by simply moving the control column back or forward. If, for any reason, the tail plane is removed then there are two effects on the stability of the aeroplane.

First, the download on the rear of the aircraft is lost causing it immediately to pitch down. If the weight of the tail plane is lost, then obviously the aircraft also becomes nose heavy and this will again cause the aircraft to pitch down into a dive. Quite likely, this violent pitching forward and down could cause a consequential structural failure of the main plane. In effect, a total disintegration of the airframe could occur, very rapidly, as a result of the loss of the tail section. This could, quite possibly, also include the separation of the engine from its firewall mountings and thus result in the descent to earth of a Spitfire in several large sections – tail, wings, fuselage and engine. In the case of W3185 we have the famous painting by distinguished aviation artist Frank Wooton titled "Bader Bale Out". In it, we see a Spitfire minus the complete tail unit from the rear fuselage aft descending in a forty-five degree dive with Bader exiting the cockpit. The reality was probably very different. Of course, as well as the airframe, we also need to look at how such mid-flight structural failures affect the pilot of the aircraft.

When an aircraft manoeuvres, as in a steep turn or a loop, the apparent mass or weight of the pilot and aircraft increases. This effect is known as "G", and can be both positive and negative. Positive G is experienced when the nose of the aircraft is pitching up, towards the pilot, and negative G when the aircraft is pitching down, away from the pilot. G is reported numerically on a simple system whereby at 2G a pilot weighs twice his normal weight and

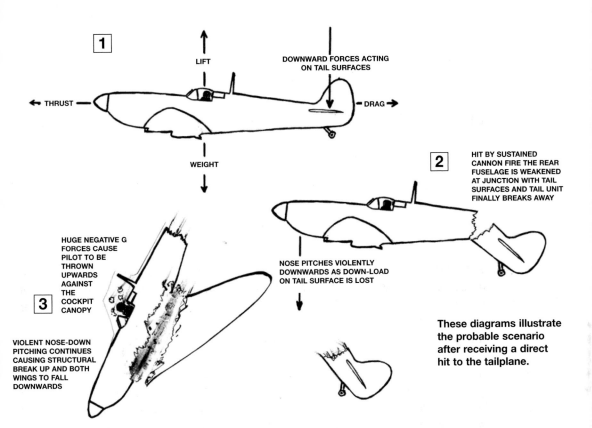

1 LIFT
DOWNWARD FORCES ACTING ON TAIL SURFACES
← THRUST
DRAG →
WEIGHT

2 HIT BY SUSTAINED CANNON FIRE THE REAR FUSELAGE IS WEAKENED AT JUNCTION WITH TAIL SURFACES AND TAIL UNIT FINALLY BREAKS AWAY

HUGE NEGATIVE G FORCES CAUSE PILOT TO BE THROWN UPWARDS AGAINST THE COCKPIT CANOPY **3**

NOSE PITCHES VIOLENTLY DOWNWARDS AS DOWN-LOAD ON TAIL SURFACE IS LOST

VIOLENT NOSE-DOWN PITCHING CONTINUES CAUSING STRUCTURAL BREAK UP AND BOTH WINGS TO FALL DOWNWARDS

These diagrams illustrate the probable scenario after receiving a direct hit to the tailplane.

at 6G he weighs six times his normal weight. When positive G is experienced, the pilot feels very heavy and the organs of his body, as well as his blood, are forced downwards. This causes the blood to drain away from the brain, leading initially to impairment of vision and, eventually, to loss of consciousness.

These effects are exacerbated by both the duration and rate at which the G is applied. Pilots can minimise the effects of positive G by tensing the leg and torso muscles, thus constricting the flow of blood in these parts of the body and thereby reducing the flow of blood away from the brain. Using these techniques, a fit young pilot can sustain 3G for some time and 6G for several seconds. In Bader's case, because he had no legs for the blood to drain into, he was at an advantage and could therefore probably sustain much higher levels of G than his contemporaries. During combat situations where he was pulling high levels of *positive* G this was clearly an advantage. However, during the episode of his bale out he would have been experiencing high levels of *negative* G. As such, his lack of lower limbs may well have been a physiological *disadvantage*.

In the case of negative G, the blood is forced into the brain and therefore tensing of the muscles has absolutely no beneficial effect. Sustained or very high levels of negative G can cause rupturing of the blood vessels in the eyes, and it is a well established fact of aviation medicine that pilots who have experienced high negative G will often have bloodshot eyes for some days after the event. Pilots can, in fact, tolerate much less negative G than they can positive G. When he is subjected to positive G a pilot is forced downwards into his seat whereas, when he experiences negative G he is thrown upwards, away from the aircraft, and is only restrained by his seat harness.

Several sources have quite erroneously stated previously that Bader's lack of legs may well have assisted his G tolerance during the incident on 9 August 1941. Clearly, that is not the case at all because he was subjected to negative G and the blood was forced upwards into his head. His limbless condition did not help him at all when his Spitfire pitched violently forward on losing its tail (or large parts thereof).

In the context of this investigation, the bloodshot eye syndrome is interesting. In the case of Bader we know from his former St Omer hospital room-mate, Justin O'Byrne, that Bader had severely bloodshot eyes upon capture. Indeed, O'Byrne's testimony is validated by a German notice issued immediately after his escape from St Omer hospital on 19 August 1941 stating that the fugitive still had a badly bloodshot right eye. Undoubtedly this was the medical consequence of high negative G, and this all begins to make sense when looking further at Bader's bale out event as well as at the experiences of two other wartime fighter pilots who found themselves subjected to extreme negative G in aeroplanes that broke up around them. The first case involves that of a Messerschmitt 109 pilot who was brought down over England during 1941.

Leutnant Julius Heger of Stab/JG 53 was shot down near Ashford, Kent, on 9 May 1941 by a Spitfire of 92 Squadron and, when hit, his aeroplane simply broke up in mid-air around him. Heger was literally thrown from the disintegrating wreckage and temporarily blacked-out before coming to and managing to deploy his parachute. Having been subjected to massive negative G forces, and injured during his involuntary ejection from the cockpit, Heger also had very severely bloodshot eyes. Writing to the author, he recalled the look of horror on the faces of the nurses who looked after him in hospital when he was captured. "The whites of my eyes," he explained, "were simply two red pools of blood."

Another pilot who had a fighter break up around him – this time a Spitfire – was Pilot Officer Keith Lawrence. Flying with 234 Squadron during the Battle of Britain, Lawrence was later posted to 421 Flight at RAF Hawkinge and it was from here, on 27 November 1940, that he was shot down. His victor was probably Leutnant Gustav "Mickey" Sprick of II/JG 26 whose cannon shells slammed into Lawrence's Spitfire exploding on the main spar near the wing-root and literally tearing the wing from the fuselage. There was a huge bang, and, in an instant, the Spitfire broke up around the young pilot who had no time for such niceties as opening the cockpit canopy, removing his flying headgear or undoing the straps.

Before he knew what had happened he had been flung through the Perspex canopy, his Sutton seat harness torn apart as he went, and the oxygen and radio leads for his helmet and mask wrenched from their sockets. The seat harness, designed to withstand huge stresses, was a substantial affair made of heavy duty canvas webbing with a reinforcing steel band running through its centre. And yet it had torn apart like paper. Such were the loadings imposed by the effects of huge negative G.

In the case of Keith Lawrence it had literally flung him out of the wreckage, although not without some personal cost in the way of injuries. Lawrence suffered a broken and dislocated right shoulder, and a badly broken right leg – its bone shattered. With a disabled right arm the stunned pilot was, at first, unable to pull the "D"-ring of his parachute located on the left side of his body but, after some desperate fumbling, he managed the feat with his left arm and drifted down to land in the English Channel. As he descended, he watched the surreal spectacle of a wing from the Spitfire he had just been flying flutter down to earth. It, and the main wreckage, struck the ground near Sholden, close to Deal. Lawrence's injured right shoulder was undoubtedly caused when the seat harness straps were broken against his body, and his right leg mangled during the ungainly ejection from the cockpit.

Although he does not report bloodshot eyes, he was without doubt flung out under massive negative G and his testimony of a Spitfire breaking up around him is certainly enlightening.

Another interesting and relevant description of the demise of a Spitfire comes from Flight Lieutenant Zurakowski of 234 Squadron who was shot down over the Isle of Wight on 24 August 1940. Hit under a weight of cannon strikes from a German fighter, Zurakowski's machine had taken substantial damage to the tail area and, losing control, he baled out as his Spitfire went into a flat spin. Zurakowski tells the story in his own words:

> I baled out at about 18,000ft when I lost all rudder and aileron control and soon found that I was descending faster than my Spitfire which was spinning above my head. I was afraid to pull the rip cord to open the parachute because that would have slowed me down, thus risking a collision with my Spitfire. The ground was approaching fast and when I could distinguish a man standing in a field with a gun I decided to pull the rip cord. It was now or never!

As the 'chute opened, it luckily yanked Zurakowski out of the way of his Spitfire which crashed into a field near the spot where he landed – the Polish pilot remarked that its speed on hitting the ground was fairly low and actual impact damage relatively minimal. Upon examination of the wreck it was found that 20mm cannon shells had caused failure of the engine mounting, one had also hit the port wing and two others had hit the fuselage/tail junction. So, interestingly, here we have a Spitfire that fell earthwards like a falling sycamore leaf and had relatively "minimal" ground impact damage. It also had its engine torn from the airframe by a combination, presumably, of combat damage and torque-like effects as it spun. It had also taken substantial tail section damage.

Putting all of this into the context of Bader's demise, then, it is much easier to see what probably happened and how it might have happened. With the initial break up of the tail section, and almost immediate loss of elevator control, the Spitfire went into an ever steepening dive. Bader, we know, spoke of the control column falling uselessly into his lap – a clear indication that the control cables to the elevators were severed. As it entered the dive, stresses on the damaged tail increased and a major portion of the tail separated from the fuselage. At this point, the negative G forces on Bader were increasing tremendously, and his vision and thinking would have become fuzzy and seriously impaired. As it pitched forward violently, the break up of the over-stressed airframe continued apace and even if Bader had already begun to prepare for evacuation in the first instant of control-loss then he may have physically been unable to get much further when the combination of total airframe failure and negative G flung him out of the cockpit. His perception of being "sucked out" would fit well the negative G effect, and the whole event may well have broken his seat harness straps too. With negative G now forcing him from the cockpit, his inert and immobile artificial leg was trapped – maybe in the remains of the flailing seat harness or somewhere under the cockpit canopy rails. In another account he talks of his flying helmet being torn from his head – a strong indicator of a pilot who was leaving in an unplanned and involuntary manner – as per Keith Lawrence!

Certainly, Bader talks of the confusion of those seconds and it is likely, for a time, he had blacked out and knew nothing of what was happening to him. Later, perhaps, he tried to make sense of those "grey" moments with his mind naturally trying to fill in the missing detail with a mixture of fact and assumption. We know for sure that upon capture he had two seriously bloodshot eyes. So, all the pieces fit but we need to bear in mind that the whole process described above was probably over in seconds rather than minutes.

If Bader's Spitfire was now falling in pieces this explains the nature of the wreckage witnesses saw on the ground, the lack of any remaining evidence at the point of impact and what Jeff West clearly saw falling erratically to earth. Equally, Bader's injuries make sense too. The bloodshot eyes, broken ribs from the breaking seat harness, cuts from the shattering Perspex and with the helmet and oxygen mask being ripped away from his head explaining, perhaps, his gashed throat? It is not, by any means, a definitive scenario but it is one that makes a great deal of sense from the assembly of all the facts we have available. Many of those "facts" are, of course, details put together from a wide range of eyewitness accounts. Many of them are contemporary, drawn from reports written or made at the time or very soon afterwards, and many post-date the crash by upwards of ten years or even more. Before finally leaving the scientific aspect of examining Douglas Bader's demise, then, we need to consider one other factor of overwhelming importance; how reliable are the eyewitnesses?

It is difficult to be prescriptive in answering this question because of the wide-ranging variables involved, but psychologist Dr Fiona Gabbert has specialised in the study of the reliability of witness statements and is able to provide us with some very generalised observations on the subject of witness accounts which make up much of the background to this book:

> If we are dealing with the memory of something that is personally important then these memories tend to be encoded at a much deeper level and rehearsed often. *(Casson's statement that he had gone over the events so often in his daydreams is a good illustration of this particular point – Author)*
>
> Of course, over time we forget some details and things become more fuzzy as opposed to the retention of all the detail. However, if these are important memories then the retention will be better than for other memories we have. Another factor is that emotionally arousing events, for example high stress situations, have the effect of focusing the person's attention towards that which is the source of arousal or stress. The outcome is that peoples' memories tend to be very good for central details of that event, i.e. what happened at the specific time of "X" happening, as opposed to what happened five minutes before or afterwards. So, on the whole, you have no real reason to doubt even the fifty-year-old statement providing that this person is recalling a personally important memory that was associated with some level or stress or arousal at the time of encoding. The only cautionary note is that some people may have embellished their memory after years of telling the same story. In other words, spiced it up a bit. Such exaggerations will then be very difficult to separate out from what really happened.

So, there we have a professional view as to how we might assess, at a very basic level, the witness statements we have. In fact, and dealing first with Bader, we have no particular reason to doubt the generalities of what he described happened to him on Circus 68. Clearly, it was a very personal event to him with no witness to verify or discount the story. However, the overall view of the general circumstances relating to the experiences of other Tangmere Wing participants is mostly mutually corroborated by all who were there. Again, we have no reason to doubt the sequence of events that day and we also have a radio chatter transcript to help us.

With Bader's account, though, this has to be tempered with the likelihood that it may have been spiced-up a little over the years. We also know that his story went from being shot down to collision, but it seems very likely that Bader's perception of what happened once he was hit and began to go down was very much how he believed things happened –

although with a strong possibility that any missing bits of detail may have been added in as embellishment but with probably no disingenuous or dishonest intent. It was perhaps just to rationalise and put straight in his own mind any aspect that he could make no sense of. As for the other contemporary accounts, (e.g. pilots' combat reports) we are seemingly faced with a different set of issues here.

Made as they were at the time, they *ought* to represent a very accurate account of what really happened if we follow Dr Gabbert's view. Clearly, though, we have a number of serious conflicts with this premise. First, we have some accounts (from both British and German pilots) of aircraft going down which bear no relation at all to the known, verifiable and established facts. Second, we have some pilots viewing the same event but in a very different manner. In dealing with the first issue, it might be relevant to look at what the New Zealand ace Al Deere had to say about things (see also Appendix H):

> ...In most cases there was no intention on the part of the pilot to mislead; it was more a case of imagination, fired up by the excitement of battle, causing him to dream up a picture....that now became an enemy aircraft destroyed.

So, perhaps it is necessary to take a benevolent view of *all* those pilots who submitted what are now shown to be "doubtful" claims that day. Possibly, just possibly, some were over-egging the pudding and gilding the proverbial lily – but we have no proof or evidence of that in relation to the specifics of combat claims during Circus 68. In all probability, each of the pilots *believed* they had seen events exactly as they had reported them and thus, following that assumption, Dr Gabbert's opinion holds good. As for different viewpoints of the same episode, then one has to look no further than present-day witness statements of road traffic accidents, or of criminal acts, that are often related through the courts to realise that there will perhaps be at least as many versions of the event as there are witnesses *to* those events!

The foregoing, then, gives an outline of what one might describe as the more "scientific" elements of Bader's loss. They are elements that need to be taken into consideration before reaching any conclusions on the matter.

CHAPTER SIXTEEN

CONCLUSIONS

The starting point for this particular journey of investigation and enquiry had been the two books *Reach for the Sky* and *The First and the Last*, both published during the 1950s. Each book relates the story of Bader's downing from entirely different perspectives; in *Reach for the Sky* we have Bader colliding with a Messerschmitt. In Galland's book we have Bader being shot down. Interestingly, Bader wrote the foreword to the English language edition of Galland's book, stating: "On 9 August 1941 I collided with one of Galland's chaps who knocked my tail off...." and yet, within the text of that very same book, Galland explains how Bader, when captured, had badly wanted to know who had shot him down! From the very outset, then, we have controversy. A difference of viewpoints. Trying to get to the truth, sorting the facts from the fiction and filling in some of the missing detail has been a challenge. Hopefully, though, this book will serve to at least help clarify what happened that day and to give a more accurate perspective as to how things really were. In summary, then, let us examine each main facet of the case and the conclusions reached by the author.

Group Captain Sir Douglas Bader CBE, KBE, DSO & Bar, DFC & Bar, Légion d'Honneur, Croix de Guerre, 1910-1982. During his later life, when this photograph was taken, Bader had begun to concede that he may after all have been shot down.

CIRCUS 68 ASSESSED

Circus 68 as a stand-alone mission was a total operational failure for the Royal Air Force. The primary target for the attacking Blenheims of Bomber Command could not be found and the bombs aimed at the secondary target near Fort Phillipe fell harmlessly in a field and in the English Channel. Fighter Command lost a total of six Spitfires destroyed, with three pilots prisoner of war and two killed. The loss of a notable RAF pilot, Bader, was a blow to both RAF and public morale and what might today be called a public relations disaster. Three of the Spitfires lost were almost certainly brought down by friendly fire. Only one Luftwaffe fighter aircraft was actually brought down by pilots of RAF Fighter Command on Circus 68 despite their total of thirteen claimed as definitely destroyed and five probably destroyed. On the other hand, the Luftwaffe fighter pilots of JG 26 claimed eight Spitfires shot down during the course of Circus 68, although their Propaganda Kompanie report stated that thirteen had actually been downed. Of the five RAF fighters actually brought down in France during Circus 68 only two were actually shot down by German pilots.

In terms of the part played by Bader and the Tangmere Wing, the absence of 41 Squadron to act as top cover undoubtedly had an impact upon the outcome of the day's events. With an unserviceable air speed indicator it would have been sensible for Bader to have personally turned back home, and to have relinquished command of the wing to Burton or Holden. It was not crucial for the operation of a wing for it to be led by its wing leader. (Indeed, the Kenley Wing was operating that day without its wing leader, Wing Commander "Johnny" Kent.) Once the enemy was sighted by the wing, Bader lost valuable minutes searching for them when others could see them. He should have sent down the section that had them in sight and retained the tactical advantage. Instead, he placed his wing at a disadvantage allowing the enemy above and behind to become an unacceptable threat.

It is the author's view that this was due to his own desire to add to his personal score. When Bader led A Flight of 616 Squadron down to attack he seems to have done so without any instruction to the rest of 616 Squadron as to whether they should follow or stay put. As a result, the remainder were left to make up their own minds and eventually, and rather haphazardly, followed Bader down in the attacking dive.

COLLISION OR SHOT DOWN?

Absolutely no hard evidence exists for a mid-air collision with a Messerschmitt 109, either in a documentary or physical sense, and we only have Bader's anecdotal account of this. If we accept that Bader's Spitfire lost much of its tail plane, then that sudden loss would result in immediate failure of any elevator control (consistent with the stick flopping loosely back into Bader's lap) and a sudden and violent forward pitching of the aeroplane. However, it is the author's view that the loss of either the whole tail plane, or large parts thereof, was caused by gunfire from another aircraft.

The dramatic effect of such a sudden and catastrophic loss of essential airframe components, and the attendant loss of control, may well have led Bader to the belief that collision was the only explanation. When captured, though, and eventually taken to the JG 26 base at Audembert, it is clear that Bader thought he had been shot down and asked to meet his victor. The collision version of events only emerges when Bader is transferred to a prisoner of war camp. There are three possible explanations for this: a) Bader has reflected on events and genuinely concludes that the only explanation is collision b) Bader prefers the collision story on arrival at the camp in order to protect his own ego amongst the other prisoners and because he considered himself too good to be shot down; and, c) Bader creates the collision story for public consumption when he writes to his journalist friend, Henry Longhurst. Again, an ego-driven move but once the story has gone public, it has to stick. Certainly, Galland, Laddie Lucas, Johnnie Johnson and Cocky Dundas all believed, and independently of each other, that Bader had been shot down. Another testimony, too, is an important one to consider.

Retired air accident investigator Bernie Forward says:

A collision with another aircraft sufficiently violent instantaneously to sever the tail of the Spitfire would have certainly involved the loss of the other aircraft due to the substantial damage that would have been caused. Since I understand that there is no evidence to support any "matching" Luftwaffe loss then this theory is dismissed.

It is the unequivocal view of the author that Bader was shot down. There was no collision.

THE BALE OUT

If we accept that, by whatever cause, Bader's Spitfire had lost much of its tail unit then there are elements of the bale out and the circumstances surrounding it that have to come under scrutiny. First, Bader says that when he looked back he saw that everything behind the radio mast had gone. In fact, it would be totally impossible to see if this was actually the case via the cockpit-mounted rear view mirror. When sitting in the cockpit of a Spitfire, it would also be impossible to see if this were the case by physically turning around – even supposing one could! It is possible that he could have seen the tips of the tail planes, fin and rudder in his mirror but, in this case there must even be some doubt about that.

In his post-war combat report, Bader modifies his account by saying that at first he thought everything aft of the radio mast had gone but, in fact, it was probably only the empennage. Clearly, Bader's physical handicap hindered his exit considerably but the frequently published suggestion that "...if he did not have artificial legs he would have died" needs to be viewed with scepticism. The inference, of course, is that it was only the breaking of the leg retention straps that saved him – although who is to say that a pilot with full use of his limbs would have been trapped in the first place?

We have seen that a complete loss of a tail section on a Spitfire would cause the aeroplane to pitch violently forward, both wings to fail downwards and then a total disintegration of the remainder to occur. All of this would have taken place in a very short time span, and would have probably resulted in the pilot being immediately rendered unconscious, or at least temporarily "greying-out", before being flung clear under negative G. In Bader's case, though, we are told of his epic struggle to exit a tail-less and plummeting Spitfire. It is the author's view that Bader lost large sections of his tail unit and all elevator control, but not initially the complete tail section and rear fuselage. Bader probably partly clawed his way and was partly flung from the cockpit of his Spitfire which was breaking up as it fell. Again, Bernie Forward is able to offer a professional view:

Damage to Bader's Spitfire due to gunfire, either cannon or machine gun, is rather difficult to quantify because of the number of variables involved. From what is recorded of the incident I consider that the following sequence best fits what we know: The rear end of the Spitfire was substantially damaged, probably severing the control cables to the elevators. This would account for the sloppy feeling of the control column. Some of the elevator was shot away causing the aeroplane to go into a dive. At this stage, the dive was possibly not too severe but sufficient to cause a significant and increasing rise in airspeed. As the speed increased in the dive so the structural loads on the rear of the aircraft would have increased dramatically eventually leading to the sudden and complete loss of the rear fuselage. At this point, further structural failures would have occurred as the aeroplane pitched violently forward and subjected high negative G on Bader.

Bader's artificial leg was found in an open field and was not "dug out" from under the wreck of the Spitfire as suggested in *Reach for the Sky*. He landed on his parachute at Rue Basse, Boeseghem, was initially picked up by civilians and then taken into custody by the Germans. His injuries included broken ribs and two very severely bloodshot eyes. Both of these conditions were the effects of being involuntarily ejected from a disintegrating aircraft. The relationship of Bader's parachute landing site with the likely crash site is significant when the scientific calculations of Bader's rate and path of descent, and also his likely exit point above ground, are all taken into account and set against each other.

CRASH OF THE SPITFIRE

Although no proof has ever been found, the most likely crash location is at Mont Dupil, Blaringhem. Strong circumstantial evidence and relatively robust information handed down from now deceased eyewitnesses adds weight to this belief. The circumstances appertaining to the two conclusions above ("Collision? Or Shoot Down?" and "The Bale Out") lead naturally to the conclusions relating to the actual crash of the Spitfire.

The newspaper article of 1945 in *L'Echo de La Lys* adds a very high degree of credible support to the deduction that wreckage of W3185 fell at Mont Dupil. If, however, the impact point of the wreckage was in the meadow indicated by M Duhamel then it might at first be considered surprising that not a single fragment of the Spitfire can now be found there. However, credible second-hand eyewitness information speaks of the two wings of the aeroplane being found in fields on the other side of the N43 from Mont Dupil and this certainly points to a mid-air disintegration either at or after the point when Bader exited the cockpit.

Bader, through *Reach for the Sky*, says that he looked for, but could not see, any burning wreckage of his Spitfire as he descended by parachute and remarked that there was "probably not enough left to burn". In this observation he may well have been very close to the truth. Whether the "wings" spoken of by witnesses were the main planes or tail planes it is impossible to assess accurately. Not only do we have the reports of aircraft wreckage at or near Mont Dupil, but an engine and propeller unit are also said by Duhamel to have fallen at the nearby Desprez sawmill.

It is the view of the author that wreckage of Spitfire W3185 did indeed fall at and around Mont Dupil and had begun to disintegrate before final impact. Indeed, the tumbling and disintegrating aircraft seen by Sergeant West was almost certainly Bader's Spitfire. Equally, the Spitfire which another French witness, Jacques Taffin, had seen fall apart in that very bit of airspace after what he described as "being hit by flak" was quite probably Bader's aeroplane, too. To M Taffin a hit by flak was probably the only way he could explain the disintegration he had seen. Separation of the wings, the engine and the fuselage in mid-air would also have resulted in the final impact of the falling wreckage being far less violent than that which would result from an aerodynamically sound aeroplane still under its own power. The result of a much less severe impact from a relatively low velocity and an almost confetti-like descent of debris could well explain the absence of any physical evidence at the Mont Dupil site today. Put simply, there was no penetration into the soil of the falling wreckage except, perhaps, the engine – although the final impact point of the Rolls-Royce Merlin near the Desprez sawmill has not been pin-pointed.

WHO SHOT BADER DOWN?

If we have dispensed with the notion that Bader's demise was the result of collision then we must again pose the question: who shot him down? None of the filed combat reports for Luftwaffe fighter pilots who were in action that day correspond with the known facts of Bader being downed. He was introduced by Galland to Oberleutnant Schmid as his "nominated" victor when visiting JG 26 at Audembert, and not to Leutnant Kosse as has been previously suggested elsewhere. Although Schmid did claim to have shot down a Spitfire that day it was almost certainly the aircraft flown by Sergeant Haydon of 452 Squadron and was definitely not Bader. Flak can be discounted as the cause of Bader's demise, as none at all was reported over the actual target area. Flak was only encountered at the coast.

Given the remarkable similarities, then, between the description given by Flight Lieutenant Buck Casson of his particular shoot down of a Messerschmitt 109 and the downing of Bader (i.e. the loss of large parts of the aeroplane's tail and its pilot struggling to get out before eventually doing so at 6,000ft), and the absolute impossibility of linking Casson's description to any German loss, it is the conclusion of the author that Douglas Bader was the victim of accidental mis-identitfication and brought down by the friendly fire of Flight Lieutenant Buck Casson.

These, then, are the primary conclusions reached by the author in respect of Douglas Bader's last fight. Nevertheless, whilst this work takes a detailed and objective look at the available evidence, definite conclusions cannot be reached in respect of all individual aspects of that day's events. What is offered to the reader is a credible explanation for many of the incidents that occurred as part of an overall operation revolving around Circus 68 on 9 August 1941. Whatever the facts, we can be certain of one thing. To a man, all of those involved that day were surely brave and courageous fliers. All of them were ordinary young men being asked to perform extraordinary deeds. Heroes if you like….but all of them fallible.

POSTSCRIPT

The televised search for the wreckage of Douglas Bader's Spitfire revealed, as we have seen in chapter thirteen, the substantial wreckage of Spitfire MA764 that Flight Sergeant Donald Bostock had baled out of on 25 November 1943. The wreckage was collected together and brought back to the UK by Wildfire TV after its recovery and was then assembled onto a wooden framework "jig" of a Spitfire; each piece of the aeroplane being fixed to the jig in its appropriate position.

Curiously, Donald Bostock and Spitfire MA764 had no part at all in the story of Douglas Bader or of Circus 68. However, as the direct result of research for this book, and the production of the Wildfire TV television documentary, they are now forever linked. Not only did both pilots share the same initials but they were associated, too, by a common thread linking them to a farm at Mont Dupil, near

(P Dimond)

Blaringhem, in the Pas de Calais.

Of the recovered wreckage, Spitfire historian Peter Arnold commented:

> The starting point for initiating a flying Spitfire project is forever getting lower, as the world-wide barrel is scraped ever cleaner. I can look back on several "digs" in the past that were so comprehensive in terms of the finds that, if recovered today, they would more than form the basis for an airworthy reconstruction had those remains been kept together as an entity. In the case of MA764, I am delighted that the recovered material was apparently not dispersed. With the added bonus of finding both the cockpit and firewall data plates, it will surely now, with a well established trail of identity provenance, take its place on the "new" airworthy Spitfire production line.

Unfortunately, Donald Bostock passed away on 24 October 1984, but his widow, Alma Bostock, was invited to visit and view the wreck of her late husband's aeroplane and enthusiastically did so in January 2006.

It was an emotional reunion, the more so because the author was able to present Alma with Donald's old flying helmet and goggles (above) – the helmet still marked with its distinctive DB lettering. Without a doubt, this particular moment was the most satisfying and rewarding aspect of the entire Bader project – and of all the research and background work that went into a project that culminated in this book.

APPENDICES

APPENDIX A

OPERATIONAL DETAILS OF CIRCUS 68

Participating wings, squadrons, aircraft and their pilots

11 Group RAF Fighter Command
Escort Wing (North Weald)
71, 222 and 111 Squadrons

71 Squadron	**Hurricanes**	**Up**	**Down**
Flt Lt A Mamedoff	Z3781	10.35	12.20
Plt Off J Flynn	Z3679	"	"
Plt Off S A Mauriello	Z5077	"	"
Plt Off C W Tribken	Z3828	"	"
Plt Off W R Dunn	Z3267	"	12.05 (RAF Manston)
Plt Off T D McKerty	Z3494	"	12.20
Flt Lt C G Peterson	Z3170	"	"
Plt Off J A Weir	Z3677	"	"
Plt Off E Q Tobin	Z3547	"	"
Plt Off V W Olson	Z3458	"	"
Plt Off W H Nichols	Z3457	"	"
Plt Off H S Fenlen	Z3335	"	"
Plt Off W R Dunn	Z3267	12.25 (Manston)	13.05 (Base)

222 Squadron	**Spitfires**	**Up**	**Down**
Sqn Ldr Love	P8644	10.30	12.15
Sgt Lewis	P8345	"	"
Flt Lt Martin	P8505	"	"
Plt Off Sanders	P8232	"	"
Plt Off Ramsey	P8383	"	"
Sgt Ptacek	P8244	"	"
Flt Lt Davies	P8235	"	"
Sgt Sharples	P8332 ZD-L	"	"
Plt Off Lyons	P8548	"	"
Sgt Rudd	P8575	"	"
Sgt Davis	P8347	"	"
Sgt Dossett	P8503	"	"

111 Squadron	Spitfires	Up	Down
Sgt Zadrobikek	P8268	10.35	12.45
Sqn Ldr McLean	P8239	"	"
Plt Off Wainwright	P7529	"	"
Plt Off Squires*	P8198	"	"
Sgt Zouhar	P8267	"	"
Sgt Caldwell	P8064	"	"
Flt Lt Brotchie	P8469	"	"
Plt Off Timmis	P7870	"	"
Plt Off Skelly	P8428	"	"
Sgt Schrader	P7528	"	"
Sgt Haine	P7824	"	"
Sgt Cooper	P7625	"	"
Wg Cdr Gillan**	P7988	"	"
Gp Capt V Beamish***	P8360	"	"

* Pilot Officer B W B Squires was lost later on 9 August 1941 at around 17.55hrs in P8198, the Spitfire he had flown that morning during Circus 68. Squires lies buried in Bergen Op Zoom Cemetery, Netherlands.

** Wing Commander John W Gillan DFC AFC was North Weald wing leader until his death on a fighter sweep on 29 August 1941 in Spitfire W3715.

*** Group Captain Victor Beamish DSO DFC was station commander at RAF North Weald and had attached himself to the North Weald Wing to fly on Circus 68.

Escort Cover Wing (Hornchurch)
403, 603 and 611 Squadrons

403 Squadron	Spitfires	Up	Down
Sqn Ldr Morris	W3446 (V)	10.40	12.25
Fg Off McKenna	P8740 (E)	"	"
Flt Lt Cathels	W3438 (G)	"	"
Plt Off Wood	P7256 (L)	"	"
Plt Off Anthony	W3573 (K)	"	"
Plt Off Gilbertson	W3114 (R)	"	"
Plt Off Waldon*	P7266 (J)	"	"
Fg Off Price	P7260 (T)	"	"
Plt Off Ford	P8744 (P)	"	"
Plt Off Ball	P8792 (Y)	"	"
Flt Lt Christmas	W3436 (X)	"	"

Note: The individual aircraft code letter for each participating aircraft of 403 Squadron is shown in brackets after the serial number. Squadron code letters for 403 were KH.

* Pilot Officer D M Waldon was missing during the afternoon action on 9 August 1941, shot down over St Omer at 17.10 hours in the Spitfire he had flown during Circus 68, P7266. His aircraft was last seen going down in flames and although captured he died in a field hospital later that day from his wounds. He is buried at Longuenesse (St Omer) Souvenir Cemetery.

603 Squadron	**Spitfires**	**Up**	**Down**
Plt Off Falconer	W3118	10.45	12.30
Plt Off Marland	R7333	"	"
Plt Off Fawkes	W3631	"	"
Sgt Paget	R7226	"	"
Sgt Nell	R7300	"	"
Sgt Cook	W3130	"	"
Fg Off Griffiths	W3379	"	"
Sgt McKelvie	R7305	"	"
Sqn Ldr Louden	P8729	"	"
Sgt Lamb	W3629	"	"
Sgt Stone	W3213	"	"
Flt Lt Walker	W3569	"	"

611 Squadron	**Spitfires**	**Up**	**Down**
Sqn Ldr Thomas	W3522	10.30	12.15
Sgt Turlington	W3442	"	"
Plt Off Duncan Smith	W3242	"	"
Sgt Evans	W3243	"	"
Plt Off Gardner	W3515	"	"
Plt Off Campbell	W3445	"	"
Plt Off Roper-Bosch	W3248	"	(RAF Gravesend)
Plt Off Van de Houart	P8780	"	"
Plt Off Lamb	W3567	"	"
Sgt Leigh	P8743	"	"
Sgt Bye	W3227	"	"
Wg Cdr F S Stapleton*		"	"

Target Support Wings (Kenley and Tangmere)
Kenley

485 Squadron	**Spitfires**	**Up**	**Down**
Sqn Ldr Knight	P7822	10.25	12.20
Flt Lt Wells	P8022	"	"
Sgt McNeil	P7626	"	"
Plt Off Francis	P7970	"	"
Sgt Griffiths	P8598	"	"
Flt Lt Norris	P7974	"	"
Sgt Sweetman	P7621	"	"
Plt Off Compton	P7538	"	"
Sgt Miller	P8025	"	"
Plt Off Barrett	P7692	"	
Sgt Rae**	P7788	"	12.40 (RAF Detling)
Plt Off McBride	P7986	"	12.20

* Stapleton was the Hornchurch wing leader and flew with his wing on Circus 68. The serial number of his Spitfire is not recorded.

** Sergeant Rae landed at RAF Detling at 12.40 before taking off from there at 13.00 and returning to base at 13.20. Rae had become separated from the squadron on the way out and was subsequently attacked three times by a Messerschmitt 109 from 16,000ft down to 6,000ft.

452 Squadron	Spitfires	Up	Down
Sqn Ldr Bungey*	P8678	10.35	12.25
Plt Off O'Byrne	P7682	"	(PoW)
Plt Off Truscott	P7973	"	12.25
Sgt Haydon	P8361	"	(killed)
Sgt Chapman	P7590	"	(killed)
Sgt Makin	P8099	"	12.45
Flt Lt Finucane	P8038	"	12.25
Sgt Tainton	P8264	"	"
Plt Off Thorold-Smith	P8381	"	"
Sgt Chisholm	P7786	"	"
Sgt Gazzard**	?	"	-

602 Squadron	Spitfires	Up	Down
Plt Off Darling	P8787	10.30	12.10
Sgt Osborne	P8574	"	"
Sqn Ldr Deere	P8724	"	12.15
Sgt Osborn	P8426	"	12.20
Plt Off Niven	AB861	"	12.15
Sgt Bell-Walker	P7601	"	"
Flt Lt Williams	P8791	"	12.10
Sgt Niven	W3641	"	12.25
Sgt Booty	P8793	"	12.10
Sgt Murray	P8799	"	11.45

Note: The leader of the Kenley Wing at this time was Wing Commander J A Kent, although he did not participate in Circus 68. On 9 August 1941 he test-flew Spitfire AB790 and carried out a cross-country flight to Heston in Spitfire P8518.

Tangmere

610 Squadron	Spitfires	Up	Down
Sqn Ldr Holden	DW-B	10.38	12.50
Flt Lt Lee-Knight	DW-L	"	"
Plt Off Stoop	DW-E	"	"
Plt Off Gaze	DW-G	"	"
Sgt Merriman	DW-J	"	"
Sgt Pollock	DW-H	"	"
Flt Lt Crowley-Milling	DW-U	"	"
Plt Off Hugill	DW-T	"	"
Plt Off Grey	DW-V	"	"
Plt Off Bartholemew	DW-Q	"	"
Sgt Richardson	DW-S	"	"
Sgt Davis	DW-N	"	"

Note: The operations record book for 610 Squadron recorded only the aircraft letters and not the serial numbers of the Spitfires flown on Circus 68.

* Squadron Leader Bungey returned from Circus 68 with cannon fire damage to his Spitfire, P8678.

** Sergeant Gazzard took off with the squadron at 10.35 and made a forced landing at Lympne, Kent, at an unknown time and with his airscrew shot away. The serial number of his Spitfire is not recorded. His was probably the lone Spitfire seen flying very slowly, and in obvious trouble, by Buck Casson.

616 Squadron	**Spitfires**	**Up**	**Down**
Wg Cdr D R S Bader	W3185 (D-B)	10.40	(PoW)

Unfortunately, the squadron operations record book (detail of work carried out) for 616 Squadron carries no data on the individual pilots or aircraft that flew on Circus 68, save for stating that in addition to Wing Commander Bader eleven aircraft took part. All aircraft are stated to have taken off at 10.40 and returned at 12.53hrs. The following limited information comprises detail of the pilots and aircraft of 616 Squadron who are known to have taken part and has been assembled from a variety of sources in addition to the sparse detail of the operations record book:

Flt Lt L H Casson	W3438	10.40	(PoW)
Sqn Ldr W Burton	"		12.53
Sgt J West	W3424	"	"
Flt Lt H Dundas		"	"
Plt Off J Johnson	W3334 YQ-F	"	"
Plt Off P Heppell	W3456	"	"
Plt Off R Marples	W3457	"	"

The identity of the other four participating pilots of 616 Squadron remains unclear at the time of writing, but may have included Sergeants Brewer, Beedham, McKee and Jenks. Among the 616 Squadron Spitfires operating that day are known to be aircraft carrying the fuselage codes YQ-R, YQ-Y, YQ-B, YQ-G and YQ-C although it is not known which was assigned to which aeroplane or pilot, although YQ-R was possibly W3424 flown by Sergeant West.

41 Squadron	**Spitfires**	**Up**	**Down**
Sqn Ldr Gaunce	P8759	10.45	12.05
Plt Off Williams	R7291	"	"
Plt Off Ranger	W3636	"	"
Sgt Rayner	R7350	"	"
Sgt Jury	W3374	"	"
Sgt Hunt	R7213	"	"
Plt Off Beardsley	W3565	"	"
Plt Off Babbage	W3634	"	"
Sgt Glen	R7307	"	"
Sgt Swanwick	P8728	"	"
Sgt Palmer	W3564	"	"
Sgt Brew	R7210	"	"

Support Wing (Northolt)
306, 308 and 315 Squadrons

306 Squadron	Spitfires	Up	Down
Flt Lt S Zieliński	P8501 UZ-J	10.40	12.30
Plt Off C Daszuta	UZ-O	"	"
Fg Off K Rutkowski*	P8382 UZ-L	"	"
Sgt A Franczak	P8325 UZ-B	"	"
Sgt O Pudrycki	UZ-C	"	"
Sgt L Kosmowski	P8567 UZ-D	"	"
Sqn Ldr J Zaremba	P8466 UZ-Z	10.45	"
Sgt H Pietrzak	P8462 UZ-M	10.45	12.30
Plt Off Z Langhamer	UZ-S	"	"
Sgt W Jasiński	P8342 UZ-N	"	"
Plt Off W Choms	P8522 UZ-W	"	"
Sgt S Wieprzkowicz	P8473 UZ-P	"	"

308 Squadron	Spitfires	Up	Down
Wg Cdr Rolski**	P8319 ZF-A	10.50	12.50
Plt Off Zbierzchowski	P7527	"	"
Fg Off Szyszka	P8694	"	"
Sgt Zieliński	P8647 ZF-Y	"	"
Flt Lt Wesolowski	P8543	"	11.25
Plt Off Retinger	P8517	"	12.50
Sqn Ldr Pisarek	P8676	"	12.45
Flt Lt Janus	P8326 ZF-F	"	"
Sgt Schiele	P8310 ZF-E	"	"
Fg Off Surma	P8317 ZF-C	"	"
Plt Off Kremski	P8318	"	12.25
Plt Off Jakubowski	P8576	"	12.40

315 Squadron	Spitfires	Up	Down
Flt Lt Szcześniewski	P8545 PK-F	10.40	13.10
Sqn Ldr Pietraszkiewicz	P8563	"	12.35
Fg Off Czerniak***	P8506	"	13.00
Sgt Adamiak	P8666	"	12.55
Plt Off Kornicki	P8540 PK-K	"	13.00
Sgt Niewiara***	P8527 PK-A	"	12.35
Flt Lt Mickiewicz	P8464 PK-W	"	12.45
Plt Off Fiedorczuk	P8670 PK-S	"	12.40
Sgt Malczewski	P8582	"	12.30
Plt Off Gil	P7613 PK-Z	"	12.20
Sgt Cwynar	P7494	"	11.20
Sgt Jaworski	P8665 PK-P	"	12.15

Plt Off Eugeniusz Fiedorczuk of 315 Squadron claimed one Messerschmitt 109 as damaged during Circus 68. Arriving back over the English Channel he was forced to crash land at Little Waldingfield in Spitfire P8670, PK-S, the aircraft being declared a write-off.
(via W Matusiak)

* Although Flying Officer Rutkowski flew on the Circus 68 operation he had, earlier that morning, been placed under open arrest charged with low flying over Ruislip Common.

** Wing Commander Rolski was the Northolt wing leader.

*** Czerniak and Niewiara were both shot down and killed during the operation flown at 17.20hrs on 9 August 1941.

2 Group RAF Bomber Command
RAF Manston

226 Squadron	**Blenheim***	**Up**	**Down**
Sqn Ldr Waddington Flt Sgt Forsyth Flt Sgt Palmer	Z7304 MQ-S	10.40	12.00
Plt Off Griffiths Plt Off Rossiter Fg Off Chapman	V6511 MQ-B	"	"
Sgt Faurot Sgt Farquhar Sgt Lees	Z7312 MQ-N	"	"
Sgt Chippendale Sgt Gatticker Sgt Topping	V6510 MQ-A	"	"
Sgt Kidby Sgt Burcher Sgt Hughes	Z7305 MQ-T	"	"

* Each Blenheim carried four 250lb general purpose bombs for Circus 68.

Appendix B

The Combat Report compiled by Group Captain D R S Bader DSO DFC on his return to the UK in 1945

Secret

Special Intelligence Form "F" And Personal Combat Report
To: HQFC (2 copies) HQ 11 Group (2 copies) OC Day Fighter Wing, Tangmere; File

Statistical

Date	(A) August 9th 1941
Unit	(B) Tangmere Wing
Type & Mark of our Aircraft	(C) Spitfire VB (*sic*)
Time Attack was Delivered	(D) About 11.10
Place of Attack	(E) South of Le Touquet
Weather	(F) Broken cloud at 12,000ft
Our Casualties – aircraft	(G) 1 Spitfire VB, cat E.
Our Casualties – personnel	(H) Pilot, Group Captain Bader, baled out safely and became Prisoner of War.
Enemy Casualties – air combat	(I) One Me 109 F destroyed, one Me 109 F probable.
Enemy Casualties – ground or sea targets	(J) Nil

General

Group Captain Douglas Bader DSO DFC was missing from a sweep carried out by the Tangmere Wing (616, 610 and 41 Squadrons) on August 9th 1941 and was captured by the enemy. He has now been repatriated and has assumed command of the Day Fighter Wing of the Central Fighter Establishment at Tangmere. He submits the following combat report and claim for one additional enemy aircraft destroyed and one probably destroyed.

Group Captain Bader states:

> We crossed the French coast south of Le Touquet with bottom squadron 616 at 26,000ft and 610 Squadron above. The wing had lost 41 Squadron after take off. Attacked a climbing formation of about twenty Me 109 Fs. I told 610 Squadron to stay put, and dived with my section on to the leading four Mes. I nearly collided with the first one at whom I was firing and had to go behind and under his tail. Continued downwards where I saw some more Me 109s. I arrived among these who were evidently not on the look-out, as I expect they imagined the first formation we attacked were covering them. I got a very easy shot at one of these who flew quite straight until he went on fire from behind the cockpit – a burst of about three seconds. In turning away right handed from this, I collided with an Me 109 which took my tail off, it appeared up as far as the radio mast but was actually probably only the empennage. This was at about 24,000ft and I do not think it did the Me 109 much good. The collision was my fault. I baled out and landed alright, and became a Prisoner of War. Note: the Germans told me later that they had shot down 26 Spitfires and lost none that day.

Claim
   1 Me 109 F destroyed
   1 Me 109 F probable
(signed) Bader
Group Captain
DFW
CFE, Tangmere, Sussex

(signed) J MacLean
Squadron Leader
Senior Intelligence Officer
CFE Tangmere

[STAMP]
INTELLIGENCE BRANCH
17 July 1945
H.Q. – F.C.

NB: Bader incorrectly identifies his aircraft as a Spitfire VB when it was, in fact, a Mk VA. He also fails to mention under "Our Casualties" the loss of Flight Lieutenant Casson.

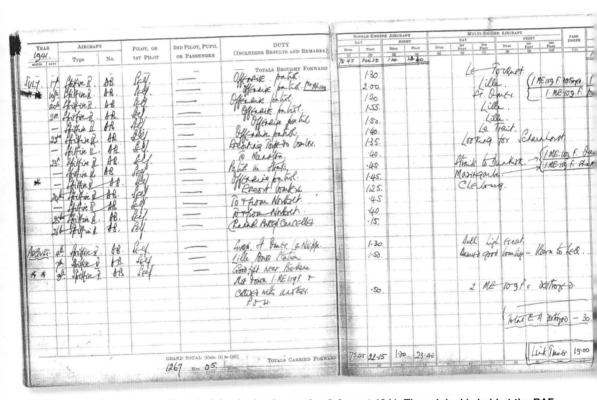

The pages from Douglas Bader's flying logbook covering 9 August 1941. The original is held at the RAF Museum, Hendon. Bader clearly completed these particular entries upon his return from captivity. It can be seen that he "confirms" his destruction of two Messerschmitt 109s in what he called a "Good fight near Béthune". The reality is that he destroyed no Messerschmitts in that combat, which is somewhat difficult to justifiably describe as a good fight! *(RAF Museum)*

APPENDIX C

THE TRANSCRIPT OF AIR MINISTRY INSTRUCTIONS TO FIGHTER COMMAND PILOTS ON THEIR DEFINING OF CLAIMS OVER ENEMY AIRCRAFT

Defining Enemy Casualties:

Destroyed

a) Aircraft must be seen on the ground or in the air destroyed by a member of the crew or formation, or confirmed from other sources, e.g. ships at sea, local authorities etc.

b) Aircraft must be seen to descend with flames issuing. It is not sufficient if only smoke is seen.

c) Aircraft must be seen to break up in the air.

Probables

a) When the pilot of a single-engined aircraft is seen to bale out.

b) The aircraft must be seen to break off the combat in circumstances which lead our pilots to believe it will be a loss.

Damaged

Aircraft must be seen to be considerably damaged as the result of attack, e.g. undercarriage dropped, engine stopped, aircraft parts shot away, or volume of smoke issuing.

APPENDIX D

COMPLETE LISTING OF LUFTWAFFE AIRCRAFT LOSSES TO ALL CAUSES ON 9 AUGUST 1941 IN THE LUFTFLOTTE 3 AREA OF OPERATIONS

Stab II/KG 40 Caudron C 445 "Goeland" W.Nr 472 Take-off accident at Friedrichshafen. 90% damage

III/KG 40 He 111 H-5 W.Nr 4082   F8+FT Missing. Hauptmann Heinrich Meyer & crew lost. 100%

II/KG 40 Do 217 E-1 W.Nr 5093 F8+EC Missing. Oberleutnant Kurt Müller & crew lost. 100%

I/JG 26 Bf 109 F 4 W.Nr 8350 Shot down by fighters near Aire. Unteroffizier A Schlager killed. 100%

II/JG 26 Bf 109 E 7 W.Nr 6494 Dived into ground. Pilot escaped by parachute. 100%

II/JG 26 Fw 190 A-1 W.Nr 024 Crash-landing at Le Bourget. 70%

III/JG 26 Bf 109 F 2 W.Nr 8305 Take-off accident at Liegescourt. 10%

Er.Gr/ JG 53 Bf 109 E 4 W.Nr 3337 Engine failure and emergency landing at La Rochelle. 95%

The above list is compiled directly from the Luftwaffe Quartermaster General's Returns for all aircraft losses in the northern France operational command area. The loss of the II/JG 26 Messerschmitt 109 E 7 (highlighted in the above list) is, arguably, an unsolved anomaly.

However, the descriptive terms used in these loss returns are very specific. If an aircraft was lost in combat then the return states this. In the case of this particular loss, all that is recorded is simply "dived into ground". This would seem strongly to indicate an accidental rather than a combat occurrence. The position of Merville is also quite a way further south than the main area of the Circus 68 action, and too far away to be relevant. Further, the pilot's name is not stated and no time is given for the incident.

Yet another indication that this loss was a non-combat event, and unrelated to Circus 68, is given in Reich Luft Ministerium Daily Results Report for 9 August 1941 (Ref RL 7/102) which lists all combat claims and losses. Under "own losses" is shown one Messerschmitt 109 only. This, presumably, relates to Schlager's Messerschmitt. The Merville incident is thus not shown in the RL7/102 list because it was non-combat linked. It is the author's view that this loss is wholly unrelated to the Circus 68 operations and can therefore be excluded.

APPENDIX E

LUFTWAFFE FIGHTER CLAIMS AGAINST CIRCUS 68

Oblt Johnannes Schmid Stab/JG 26 11.25hrs

Flying a Messerschmitt 109 F 4, Schmid saw Galland shoot at a single Spitfire and went with him as the geschwader kommodore attacked. As he was pulling away he saw another Spitfire flying alone which he attacked twice from behind shooting at a distance of 80-50 metres. He shot this Spitfire down using sixty cannon and two hundred and forty rounds of machine-gun ammunition in a battle which took place at 2,500 metres (8,200ft) and 10km to the east of St Omer. He saw flames with dark plumes of smoke coming off the 'plane. He saw the pilot bale out with a parachute, but didn't see where the aircraft impacted because of the clouds. His witness, Unteroffizier Richter, says that he saw the parachute of the pilot opening and saw the aeroplane go down to the north of St Omer on the edge of a forest. He saw the crash site because after the attack he lost Schmid in the clouds, went down below them and then flew north at a height of just 300 metres (1,000ft).

There seems little doubt, then, that Schmid had shot down Sergeant Haydon of 452 Squadron. He fell dead with a partly opened parachute and his aircraft crashed in the Forest of Tournehem. The time, geographical location and circumstances fit exactly with all the known facts of Haydon's loss.

Unteroffizier Heinz Richter Stab/JG 26 11.30hrs

Richter was flying a Messerschmitt 109 F. After Schmid's attack, Richter lost Schmid in the clouds. He then flew away from St Omer at 300 metres and saw a Spitfire flying at the same height. He veered to the left to recognise it better and then flew behind it at a height of 350 metres (1,150ft) until 75 metres away and shot at the cockpit from above and behind. The Spitfire began to nose dive immediately and fell into the sea near Dunkirk. He presumed the pilot was killed.

It is impossible to match any RAF loss on Circus 68 with Richter's claim.

Obstl Adolf Galland – Stab/JG 26 11.32hrs
Galland attacked a Spitfire at 4,000 metres (13,000ft) north-west of St Pol. He attacked the aircraft from behind and below using one MG 151 20mm cannon and two engine cowling mounted MG 131s (12.7mm)* at a distance of one hundred down to twenty metres. Parts of the 'plane came off from around the fuselage and the aircraft dived into the water, the pilot baling out and landing close to Cumole(?) – *sic*.

It is impossible to match any RAF loss during Circus 68 with Galland's claim.

Lt Wolfgang Kosse 5/JG 26 11.40 – 11.45hrs
Very little information on this "kill" is recorded and two different German primary sources give differing times – 11.40 and 11.45hrs. We do know that the attack took place at 3,000 metres (10,000ft) in the St Omer region.

It is difficult to tie this into any specific RAF loss, but Kosse may possibly have attacked Sergeant Haydon's Spitfire as well as Schmid. Truscott reported they were attacked at about 10,000ft and noticed Haydon had vanished by 11.25. Possibly, Haydon got split up from his squadron, and maybe hit, which was when Schmid picked him off as a singleton. It is otherwise impossible to tie this reported victory into any other RAF loss.

Ofw Walter Meyer 6/JG 26 Between 11.25 and 11.30
Very little detail is recorded for this claim, except that Meyer shot down a Spitfire between these times near St Omer.

Given the lack of detail it is impossible to tie this claim to any of the RAF losses. We can, though, rule out Casson and Haydon. In theory, the time and location could fit Pilot Officer O'Byrne, Sergeant Chapman or Wing Commander Bader.

Ofw Erwin Busch 9/JG 26 11.25hrs
Again, very little detail is recorded except that Busch downed a Spitfire at this time in an unknown location.

As with Meyer's claim, it is impossible to fit this reported "kill" to any specific RAF loss although, again, O'Byrne, Chapman or Bader could theoretically have been his victim.

Oblt Erwin Biedermann 9/JG 26
Very little detail is recorded, except that Biedermann claimed to have downed a Spitfire on this day at an unknown time and in an unknown location.

Without knowing the time or location of this claim it is impossible conclusively to tie this to the Circus 68 action. It is possible the victory was claimed in the afternoon battle, although it is, of course, equally possible for it to have been during the Bader action – in which case, and with such scant information available, Biedermann could well have attacked any of the Spitfires lost on Circus 68.

---

* The armament cited here is interesting in that both Galland and Bader had "issues" relating to the armaments of their respective fighters. Galland felt strongly that the Me 109 F was under-armed and therefore had the weaponry of three of his personal aircraft increased, the aeroplane he was flying on 9 August 1941 being one of these "specials". Conversely, Bader was averse to flying cannon-armed Spitfires and thus had sought out his own personal Spitfire VA with its armament of eight .303 Browning machine guns.

Hptm Gerhard Schoepfel
A full account of Schoepfel's combat is given in chapter five.

There is no doubt that Schoepfel shot down Buck Casson, although there are some slight discrepancies in the locations given. Casson says it was ten miles south of Calais, Schoepfel that it was east of Marquise. German ground reports give Les Attaques as the crash location. As this is about ten kilometres south-east of Calais and to the north-east of Marquise it is reasonable to assume that Les Attaques is the exact location.

In addition to the above claims by Luftwaffe fighter pilots, flak batteries situated at Le Portel (near Boulogne) and Sangatte (near Calais) claim to have brought down a total of three British aircraft into the sea during the Circus 68 action.

No RAF losses match these claims by anti-aircraft units. There was flak reported over the coast on the way in and out, but none over the target area. Several RAF pilots reported heavy flak on the way back out which followed them some distance out to sea.

APPENDIX F

RAF LOSSES ON 9 AUGUST 1941 DURING CIRCUS 68

616 Squadron Spitfire Va W3185 "Lord Lloyd" Codes: DB Wg Cdr D R S Bader DSO DFC
Pilot prisoner of war after baling out and landing at Boeseghem. Aircraft probably that which fell at Mont Dupil near Blaringhem.

616 Squadron Spitfire Vb W3458 "Mirfield" Flt Lt L H Casson DFC
Pilot prisoner of war after being shot down by Hauptmann G Schoepfel of JG 26. Crash-landed 800 metres south-west of Les Attaques and set on fire by Casson.

452 Squadron Spitfire IIA P7682 Plt/Off J H O'Byrne (RAAF)
Pilot baled out and prisoner of war, landing by parachute at Coubronne. The crash location of Spitfire P7682 has not been determined. Suggestions that the crash site was at St Martin, to the north of Aire-sur-la-Lys, are unconfirmed. In any event, given O'Byrne's known parachute landing site and the wind direction on 9 August 1941 the likelihood is that his Spitfire fell somewhere to the NNW of Coubronne as it was last seen spiralling vertically downwards and on fire. The possibility that it then travelled over twelve kilometres to the south is extremely remote. It is likely that O'Byrne was shot down by friendly fire.

452 Squadron Spitfire IIA P7590 Sgt G B Chapman
Pilot killed when his aircraft was shot down at the village of Salperwick. He was almost certainly shot down by friendly fire. Chapman lies buried at Longuenesse (St Omer) Souvenir Cemetery.

452 Squadron Spitfire IIA P8361 "Krakatoa" Sgt G B Haydon
Pilot shot down by Oberleutnant Schmid of Stab/JG 26. Aircraft crashed at Forêt de Tournehem. Sgt Haydon baled out but fell dead in a tree near the village of Quercamps. Haydon lies buried at Longuenesse (St Omer) Souvenir Cemetery.

315 Squadron Spitfire IIA P8670 "Second City of London Textile"
Codes: PK – S Plt/Off Fiedorczuk
Pilot crash-landed unhurt at Little Waldingfield, Suffolk, due to lack of petrol on returning from Circus 68. Aircraft was struck off charge on 14 August 1941 as it had been damaged beyond repair.

There were no losses, or reported damage, to the participating aircraft of 266 Squadron. Later in the day, RAF Fighter Command suffered a further five losses over the continent:

    Plt Off W B Squires,111 Squadron, Spitfire P8198 (Killed)
    Fg Off J M Czerniak, 315 Squadron, Spitfire P8506 (Killed)
    Fg Off A Niewiara, 315 Squadron, Spitfire P8696 (Killed)
    Plt Off D M Waldon, 403 Squadron, Spitfire R7266 (Killed)
    Plt Off A Nitelet, 609 Squadron, Spitfire W3254 (Evaded – ret to UK)

Some of the above five casualties have previously been linked to Circus 68, although all of them were in fact lost on an unrelated operation later that same day.

Appendix G

Transcript of R/T transmissions by the Tangmere Wing during Circus 68

Beachy Head RAF Wireless Monitoring Station

To	From	Time of Origin	Message
Woody	DB	11.01	This is the most obvious farce I have ever seen in my life.
DB	Woody	-	Your message understood.
Ken	DB	-	Are you OK?
DB	Ken	-	Yes.
Ken & Elmer	DB	-	Start getting height as quick as you can now will you?
DB	Ken	-	Elmer's not with us.
DB	Elmer	-	---- ? ---- (unintelligible)
Elmer	DB	11.04	Cannot understand what you say but we're on our way. If you're not with us you'd better decide for yourself whether to come or go back.
DB	Elmer		Unreadable XMN.
DB	Ken	11.05	Making smoke.
Ken	DB	-	Levelling out. I'm going down very slightly.
DB	Ken	-	OK
	DB	11.07	KSL you don't see them very well against this stuff.

Walker L	Beetle	11.08	DB is twenty miles ahead of you.
Beetle	Walker L	-	Message understood.
-		-	I think I see trails above and on our left.
?	Ken	11.10	Yes I have seen 'em.
			I think we might get up a bit.
			I think it was very ? that trail we made.
Walker 1 & 2	?	-	Unreadable XMN.
DB	Woody	-	There are 2+ five miles to the east of you.
Woody	DB	-	OK. That transmitter is quite impossible.
			Please use the other.
DB	Woody	-	OK. Is this better?
Woody	DB	-	Perfect.
DB	Ken	-	Throttle back a bit I can't keep up.
Ken	DB	-	Sorry my ASI is U/S.
			Throttling back.
-	DB	-	I will do one circle left now quickly.
DB	Woody	-	There are now 20+, no height, five miles east of you.
Woody	DB	11.12	That's getting better. OK.
-	Roy	-	There's three coming down astern of us now. I'm keeping my eye on them.
Roy	-	-	OK.
-	Roy	-	Sorry there's now six. Open out a little.
-	Roy	-	I make it eleven now.
Roy	-	-	Cut out the running commentary and just let us know where they are.
DB	-	-	Smoking.
Ken	DB	-	Circling left.
DB	Beetle	-	There are 40+ fifteen miles to the NE of you.
Beetle	DB	-	Are our friends where they ought to be? I haven't much idea where I am.
DB	Beetle	-	Yes, you are exactly right and so are your friends.
Walker 3	-	-	Take it easy will you?
		11.14	Aircraft at nine o'clock a little above over the smoke trail.
DB	Roy	11.16	Keep turning left and you'll see aircraft at nine o'clock.
Ken	DB	-	Can you see those or is it yourself?
DB	-	-	Look beneath you over the cloud.

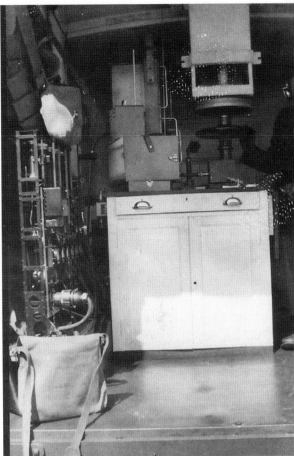

The Beachy Head radio station that monitored the R/T chatter from the Tangmere Wing during Circus 68.

The inside of the direction-finding caravan and the place where the handwritten log of the Tangmere radio transmissions was recorded.

-	DB	-	Well you tell me where to look!
DB	-	-	Underneath Billy's section now.
-	DB	-	OK I've got 'em.
			Two XMNS together.
			There's plenty of time. Get in formation.
			Straight underneath you.
Stan	DB	-	Are you OK? Are you with us?
DB	Stan	11.20	Just above you.
Crow	-	-	Keep me in sight.
			Two XMNs together.
			Unreadable XMN.
Elfin	-	-	Aircraft on our right.
Ken	DB	-	Look out for right.
Crow	-	-	Is that you behind me to the left?
-	-	-	Stay with me that aircraft at front turning left.

YQ-R	DB	-	Stay with me. (The last transmission from Douglas Bader – estimated @ 11.23)
-	-	-	Several XMNs together.
Elfin	-	-	Aircraft behind us a little to the left. Join up. Join up.
-	Rusty L	-	Join up.
Walker L	Walker 2	11.24	Aircraft two o'clock down. Big (??) here and some buggers coming down behind us. Turn port. They're coming down behind. PORT that aircraft. I'll weave about over you.
Walker 1	?	-	They're 109s all right.
Crow	-	-	One circle starboard now.
-	-	11.26	Line astern.
Walker L	Walker 3	11.27	Squadron about A.20.
Walker 3	Walker L	-	OK.
YQ aircraft	-	-	109s coming down again. Form up with YQ-C. You'll form a four. Come on. I'm on your left here.
Beetle	Rusty B3	11.28	RURM. Get into formation or they'll shoot the fucking lot of you down.
Crow	-	-	Turn port. I'll follow you.
-	Crow	-	Above or below this cloud?
YQ-R	-	-	Throttle back.
DB	Beetle	-	Withdraw now.
-	Crow	-	Two buggers just above now. Unreadable XMN. Several XMNs together.
YQ-Y	-	11.30	Get onto my port, other side of YQ-R.
Tony	-	-	Can you see it? Reform. Who the fucking hell is (???) tracer bullets? (Interference)
Tony	-	-	Are you going out now?
-	Tony	-	Yes. What is that behind me? There's about four just above the misty cloud behind. I think they're Spits. Yes. They're all Spits.
All Beetle a/c	Control	11.33	Make your way out now. Are you turning left? Just going out now.

Jimmy	-	-	Turning left.
DB	Beetle	-	Withdraw as soon as you like.
Beetle	-	11.35	We all heard it.
			Pretty good too.
			Break right.
Billy	-	-	If you can bring your squadron to starboard this time to get back.
			There's difficulties.
YQ-R	-	-	Go under this cloud and seek refuge Spitfire. Go under the cloud with me.
			Everybody with us?
			One short.
			Who?
-	-	11.38	Go under.
Jimmy	-	-	Watch the sun now Jimmy.
			OK.
			Look out.
			When do you want to break?
Elfin	-	-	Keep watching the sun.
-	-	11.40	OK. Spitfires. OK.
Crow	-	11.41	Keep fairly close. I'm going to look round by the coast.
-	Crow	-	Coming in behind you.
Jimmy	-	11.42	Unreadable XMN.
-	-	-	109 coming up on your right.
-	-	-	Who the hell's talking to whom?
			Join up boys.
Crow	-	-	Are you still about?
-	Crow	-	I'm right behind you.
Crow	-	-	Good show.
YQ	-	-	Are you going to B?
Tony	-	-	Are you going out? I've lost you. We're low down and we wouldn't see anything in any case.
-	-	11.45	Look out to the left.
Tony	Roy	11.46	Throttle back a bit.
Roy	Tony	-	OK Sorry.
			Single Spitfire flying on my left turn starboard and follow me.
DB	Beetle	11.47	Do you want any assistance?
Walker L	Beetle	-	Do you want any assistance?
Beetle	Walker L	-	Received your message. We are OK.
Elfin L	Beetle	-	Do you want any assistance?
Beetle	Elfin L	-	No. I am OK.

| Rusty L | Beetle | - | Do you want any assistance? |
| DB | Beetle | 11.49 | Are you OK? |

This was the last call to DB. There was no reply. Transmissions from the Tangmere Wing continued up until 12.24 when the last of the stragglers got home.

Key to abbreviations, names etc used in above transmissions:

Woody:	Group Captain A B Woodall, station commander, RAF Tangmere
Beetle:	Tangmere ops room
DB:	Douglas Bader (Dogsbody)
Ken:	Squadron Leader Ken Holden, CO 610 Squadron
Elfin:	610 Squadron (Elfin L = Elfin Leader)
Elmer:	Squadron Leader Elmer Gaunce, CO 41 Squadron
Walker:	41 Squadron (Walker L = Walker Leader)
Billy:	Squadron Leader Burton, CO 616 Squadron
Rusty:	616 Squadron (Rusty L = Rusty Leader)
Crow:	Flight Lieutenant Crowley-Milling, 610 Squadron
Jimmy:	Unidentified
Tony:	Flight Lieutenant Tony Lee-Knight, 610 Squadron
Stan:	Unidentified (Previous suggestions that this was Stan Turner of 145 Squadron are clearly incorrect as 145 Squadron were no longer part of the Tangmere Wing)
A20:	Angels 20 (twenty thousand feet)
RURM:	Are you receiving me?
XMN:	Transmission
KSL:	Keep sharp lookout
YQ:	Squadron fuselage codes for 616 Squadron

(Although not used in these particular transmissions, Le Touquet was given the codeword "Golf Course" in reference to the grass-covered dunes along the coast near there. St Omer was "Big Wood", a reference to the large Forêt de Clairmarais.)

Incredibly, the radio log from the Beachy Head monitoring station was picked up by a young RAF airman, James Donne, amongst scattered debris after the station had been bombed in 1943 and it was saved by him from destruction on a bonfire. The log's hard-backed air ministry-stamped covers had been blown off and one or two pages lost but the log was otherwise intact. During the 1980s the late James Donne, a friend of the author, asked what he should do with the document. The author recognised the incredible historical significance of the entries for 9 August 1941 and suggested this valuable artefact be presented to the RAF Museum, which was duly done. By great good fortune the logbook was the very one containing transcripts of all the radio chatter from the Tangmere Wing during the course of Circus 68. It is remarkable in that it is quite probably the only surviving radio transcript log for the whole of RAF Fighter Command during WW2, and doubly remarkable, surely, in that it should cover this historic episode.

APPENDIX H
RAF FIGHTER COMMAND CLAIMS DURING CIRCUS 68

Notwithstanding the instructions laid down for claiming aircraft destroyed, damaged or probably destroyed during combat (Appendix C) there was certainly a high degree of over-claiming by the participating wings during Circus 68. This was not uncommon during World War Two fighter operations and, as will be seen from Appendix E, the Luftwaffe over-claimed on this day, too. A trawl through the many thousands of pilot's combat reports held in the national archive reveals countless inexplicable or unverifiable accounts. 9 August 1941 was no exception. Indeed, some post-war analysts have concluded that during the Battle of Britain, for instance, RAF fighter squadrons were over-claiming from anywhere in the spectrum between ratios of 5:1 and 2:1. Whatever the true figure, over-claiming by fighter pilots of all nationalities and air-arms is a well accepted feature of aerial warfare by today's historians.

It is with this caveat set against claiming that we must thereby view the substance of each claim submitted by RAF (and Luftwaffe) pilots during Circus 68 operations. However, some difficulties arise in stating definitively the actual totals claimed by the various participating wings and squadrons as different RAF records present slightly different tallies. Finally, it should also be borne in mind that intercepts of the German "Enigma" codes enabled Luftwaffe casualties and losses to be accurately assessed at the highest level of British command although, naturally, any detailed knowledge of the true attrition rate for the Luftwaffe which had been gleaned did not filter down to squadron level within the RAF. Thus, all claims submitted by individual squadron intelligence officers were allowed to stand, the IO having been the final arbiter as to whether a claim for "Destroyed", "Damaged" or "Probably Destroyed" should be allowed, granted as a "shared" claim between two or more pilots, or disallowed.

North Weald Wing Claims
71 Squadron – 1 Messerschmitt 109 destroyed
222 Squadron – No claims
111 Squadron – 1 Messerschmitt 109 probably destroyed 1 Messerschmitt 109
    damaged
Plus: 1 Messerschmitt 109 destroyed by Group Captain V Beamish, officer commanding RAF North Weald

Hornchurch Wing Claims
403 Squadron – 1 Messerschmitt 109 probably destroyed
603 Squadron – No claims
611 Squadron – No claims

Kenley Wing Claims
485 Squadron – No claims
602 Squadron – 1 Messerschmitt 109 probably destroyed, 2 Messerschmitt 109s
    damaged
452 Squadron – 5 Messerschmitt 109s destroyed

Tangmere Wing Claims

610 Squadron – No claims

616 Squadron – 4 Messerschmitt 109s destroyed, 1 Messerschmitt 109 probably destroyed

41 Squadron   – No claims

Northolt Wing Claims

306 Squadron – No claims

308 Squadron – No claims

315 Squadron – 1 Messerschmitt 109 destroyed, 3 Messerschmitt 109s probably destroyed

Note: The claims listed above are extrapolated from the Headquarters, 11 Group, Fighter Command, operations record book for 9 August 1941. There is, however, some confusion and ambiguity relating to some of these claims, especially for 111 Squadron, during Circus 68.

APPENDIX I

WEATHER DATA FOR SATURDAY 9 AUGUST 1941 AT 11.30HRS FOR POSITION 50.7N 2.4E

Height	Direction/Speed (knots)	Probable Range
Surface	300/12	290-310/10-15
1,000ft (305m)		
1,640ft (500m)	320/20	310-330/15-25
2,000ft (610m)	330/15-20	320-340/15-25
3,000ft (910m)		
3,280ft (1,000m)	310/20	290-320/15-25
4,000ft (1,220m)		
4,920ft (1,500m)	290/20	280-300/15-25
5,000ft (1,520m)		
6,000ft (1,830m)		
6,560ft (2,000m)	300/20	290-310/15-25

The above data is based on weather charts for the approximate time of Bader's bale out and are shown from ground level up to the approximate height at which Bader exited his Spitfire.

Estimated cloud conditions for the above location and time*

Total cloud amount: 5 to 7/8ths

Low cloud: 1/8th cumulus (fair weather). Base approx 2,000-3,000ft

Medium level cloud: 5 (possibly 6)/8ths altocumulus/altostratus layer. Base 6,000-7,000ft

High cloud: Cirrus above 16,000ft. (No other detail available)

Data compiled by meteorological office senior forecaster, J J Allen, 11 October 2005. This information was used to help analyse weather conditions (cloud cover and levels) during the Circus 68 combats and to calculate the path of descent of Bader's parachute (wind speed and direction).

* Note: the cloud cover estimates are expressed here in eighths which is the present-day international meteorological standard although wartime reports always expressed cloud cover in tenths which was then the standard of the day.

Appendix J

Spitfire losses in St Omer region related to the "Bader search"

The downing of six other Spitfires within the immediate vicinity of the St Omer region, and the immediate locality of the supposed Bader crash area, had to be considered in respect of the intended positive identification of the crash site of W3185. Each in turn had to be eliminated as the potential site where the Bader Spitfire fell. The details of each case are as follows:

Spitfire IIA P7682 452 Squadron RAAF Pilot Officer J H O'Byrne
The circumstantial report by the officer commanding 452 Squadron stated:

> Whilst operating with Circus 68 over France on 9 August 1941 I was Blue one and Pilot Officer O'Byrne in aircraft Spitfire IIA P7682 was Blue two. During an engagement with a number of enemy aircraft I saw Pilot Officer O'Byrne's aircraft going down with smoke pouring from it. I was unable to find out that any other pilots witnessed the incident.

We are fortunate that Justin O'Byrne left a detailed written testimony of his experiences that day:

> "Nine o'clock above! Squadron break!" These were the last words I heard over my radio on the morning of 9 August 1941. The game was on in deadly earnest, and our position as top cover in the escort of the Blenheims to bomb Béthune aerodrome (*sic*) was giving to us the opportunity we had wished for to mix it rough with Jerry. Our squadron was the first Australian fighter squadron formed in England from trainees of the Empire Training Scheme and every pilot in the squadron was keen and raring to go.
>
> The sun was practically overhead as we turned and climbed to make height, and during our climb several more formations of Jerries came into view. On my left, leading Red section, was "Paddy" Finucane, our flight commander, and in the lead Squadron Leader Bob Bungey was taking the squadron into attack. There were nine Me 109s turning away to the north and I saw Finucane and Bluey Truscott engaging with their sections, guns blazing, and one 109 burst into flames and dive in. From the right, another Jerry formation came forward to attack and had been engaged. I turned in to attack a 109 diving down and away, and gave him a long burst which knocked great chunks out of his wing, fuselage and tail unit. As I turned away and started to climb again for height another Me 109 attacked me from my blind quarter and gave me the works. I caught it in the wing and fuselage and my elevator controls were out of action. I had got a piece of shell splinter in my ankle which went into my Achilles tendon and another piece made a furrow, fortunately only skin deep, on my head. By this time the glycol fumes and fire in the bottom of the cockpit had made it impossible for me to do anything but bale out. I jettisoned the canopy top of my cockpit, undid my straps and gave a tug on my seat adjuster and shot out of the old kite with such speed that I left my flying boots and socks behind.
>
> As soon as I felt sure I was clear of the tail unit I started to make up my mind about the urgent need of trying out my parachute drill. My old brain was a bit slow ticking over at this moment as so much had happened in such a short space of time.

I pulled the cord and looked up and sure enough the old silk started to take shape. I was a bit scared for a few moments as the seat-type parachute looked so small. I thought that perhaps it was only the pilot 'chute (the small handkerchief-sized parachute which is opened by a spring and pulls the main 'chute out of the container). However, I soon had to resign myself that this was all I had with which to lower myself to Mother Earth. I started swinging violently and pulled the appropriate strings to steady me down.

Whilst I was doing this I also found out that I could use the same technique for side-slipping. The air was full of dogfights and I could see several other parachutes coming down, both German and ours. I could see that I was going to land very near to a village so I tried to side-slip away from it. When I got nearer the ground I got more of an idea of my speed of drop and by now realised that I must be ready for meeting Mother Earth.

My luck in landing in a vegetable bed enabled me to protect my wounded leg and within a few minutes several French people ran over from the village to me. They were quite willing to help me, but within two or three minutes a German "polizei" came up covering me with a revolver. It was then that the horrible thought passed through my mind – "My God! I am a prisoner of war!" The policeman was then joined by three soldiers, and one of them who spoke a little English said, "For you the war is over!"

The village nearby was named Coblain (sic) and was about fifteen kilometres south of St Omer. I was taken into a French café where the French were permitted to bathe my head and foot, and one of them gave me a glass of brandy. I was taken by car to St Omer where I was placed in hospital and a German doctor started on the job of fishing out the pieces of shell from my foot.

With this information, the starting point of the quest was obviously the village of "Coblain". Unfortunately, no such village name was found to exist although a village called Coubronne was identified, and this is situated about twelve kilometres south-south-east of St Omer. It was the only possibility. Fortunately, the hunch was an accurate one and in Coubronne there were locals still living who recalled that villagers Arnaud Barbet, Paul Bertin and Jean Buire were first on the scene when an RAF pilot came down by parachute into the watercress beds (cressonière) between Quiestède and Coubronne. They recalled that the Germans arrived just as the three Frenchmen were helping the pilot, who was then taken off to the nearby village of Ecques and given a drink of brandy. There can be no doubt, then, that this was O'Byrne since all of these facts fit his personal account almost exactly.

As to the crash site of his Spitfire, some local researchers have previously suggested that a crash at St Martin, north of Aire-sur-la-Lys, could have been O'Byrne's Spitfire. René Dewasmes was a nine-year-old living nearby and playing with friends René and André Meunier when he saw an aircraft crash in flames near the Aire gravel pits. However, no evidence exists to link this with either O'Byrne or any of the other Circus 68 losses. Indeed, given the wind speed and direction at that time, and O'Byrne's now firmly established landing place, it seems highly unlikely that his Spitfire would have crashed some twelve kilometres away to the south-east! A more likely crash location would be to the north-north-west of Coubronne, and most probably somewhere in the locality of the village of Heuringhem.

Spitfire IIA P7590 452 Squadron Sergeant G B Chapman
The circumstantial report by the officer commanding 452 Squadron stated:

> Whilst operating with Circus 68 over France on 9 August 1941 at about 11.20hrs in aircraft P7590 Sergeant Chapman was Black one. Sergeant Makin was Black two and during an engagement with a number of Me 109s he saw the tail of Sergeant Chapman's aircraft shot off and the aircraft went down. No other pilots have any knowledge of this occurrence.

Sergeant Chapman was killed and the Missing Research and Enquiry Unit of the RAF which investigated Chapman's loss at the end of the war said that his aircraft had crashed at the village of Salperwick. German records confirmed that the crash site was one kilometre north-west of St Omer and this corresponds exactly with the geographical location of Salperwick.

The fact that Sergeant Chapman's aircraft was seen going down with "its tail shot off" obviously cannot be ignored in the context of this research. However, the detail of Sergeant Makin's personal report is a little more specific and describes the top half of Chapman's rudder being missing, and the port tail plane gone. Makin followed Chapman as he broke gently away from the formation with his hood open. He was seen to be flying perfectly level and do a steady turn to the left. At this point, Makin was then distracted and lost sight of Chapman. Interestingly, Makin's report goes on to say: "We were then attacked by six aircraft out of the sun *which were later identified as Spitfires*". Here, in a contemporary official report relating to fighter operations during Circus 68, we have irrefutable and significant evidence of Spitfires engaging Spitfires.

The RAF's MREU team visited Salperwick on 21 September 1946 and found witnesses to the crash who told of the Spitfire flying very low over the village when the pilot suddenly pulled up into a climb and then jumped out at around five hundred feet. Unfortunately, his parachute didn't open and he fell to his death in Salperwick village where his body was found by the mayor. The mayor reported that Chapman had suffered a fractured skull and had been killed instantly. Before the Germans came to remove the body he managed to retrieve a knife on which were engraved the initials CBGC and this was handed over to the Missing Research & Enquiry Unit's investigating officer.

Spitfire IIA P8361 "Krakatoa" 452 Squadron Sergeant G B Haydon
The circumstantial report by the officer commanding 452 Squadron states:

> Whilst operating with Circus 68 over France on 9 August 1941 at about 11.20 hours in aircraft P8361 Sergeant Haydon was Green two. Green one was Pilot Officer Truscott who reports that during an engagement with a number of Me 109s at about 10,000ft he suddenly missed Sergeant Haydon who had disappeared from his view. No other pilots on this operation noticed his absence from the flight.

The Missing Research and Enquiry Unit investigation into the loss of Sergeant Haydon found the scene of the crash to be in the Forêt de Tournehem. The cemetery records at Longuenesse St Omer, where Haydon lies buried, state the place of death to be Quercamps – although this was probably because the crash was actually nearer to Quercamps village than to Tournehem, although not actually in the Quercamps commune. Haydon, when he was found, had grievous injuries, which included a severed leg and a very badly cut face.

The following losses were all in the immediate vicinity although not on 9 August 1941. Their crash sites needed to be ruled in or out of the hunt for Bader's aircraft.

Spitfire VB BM303 611 Squadron, 8 June 1942, Sergeant J E Misseldine
The circumstantial report by the officer commanding 611 Squadron states:

> Sergeant Misseldine took off from Kenley at 13.00hrs on 8 June 1942 with eleven other aircraft of this squadron on a fighter diversion over Sangatte, St Omer and Gravelines. He was flying as Blue four. Over St Omer at 17,000ft about twenty Focke Wulf 190s were sighted below and the squadron went down to attack. Several pilots saw a pilot without a tail spinning down and confirm that the pilot baled out and landed near St Omer.

Once again, we have a tail-less Spitfire evidently coming down in the Bader crash area (albeit at a much later date) but which might reasonably have been expected to add some confusion to any eyewitness accounts emerging from local enquiries about Bader. As it happened, only one witness (Georges Goblet) was able to pinpoint the crash site and he was positive that this was Jack Misseldine's Spitfire. Certainly, we know that Misseldine landed by parachute nearby and this is confirmed in his MI9 debrief:

> I was shot down about 14.00hrs and came down by parachute near the village of Steenbecque, south-east of St Omer. I was dazed on landing, and could not get away before a hostile crowd had gathered, apparently under the impression I was a German. I managed to explain that I was British and, after hiding my equipment in a ditch, I made for a wood. On the way a young man overtook me and said he would meet me in the wood at 18.00hrs. I hid in the wood, and at 23.00hrs the man brought me food, took me by a roundabout way to the back of the village, and hid me in a chicken coop.

> I remained there for two days, sleeping on a trestle bed, and food was brought to me by the young man and also by a girl and her father. About midnight on 10 June the young man took me to a house in the village of Haverskerque to a woman who, he said, spoke English. The woman was very frightened and would not take me in, so I hid in the adjoining Forêt de Nieppe. At 18.00hrs on 11 June a young girl on a bicycle brought me a set of clothes and took me to her home at Aire-sur-la-Lys. I remained there for about three weeks until 29 June, and a doctor treated me for burns on my face.

Jack Misseldine's subsequent adventure was an extraordinary one as he was helped to escape across France and eventually made it to Gibraltar, and then home to the UK on 8 September 1942. It had been his first operational flight, and a memorable one at that! In the context of this story, however, it was clear that Misseldine's aeroplane had crashed not far from Steenbecque, and the site which Goblet had pointed out was just a short distance away from there on the road between Blaringhem and Sercus.

Georges Goblet also recalled that the pilot had landed in the Steenbecque direction. During the excavation of the crash site indicated by M Goblet nothing was found that might positively identify the aeroplane as BM303. However, a component part of a cannon-armed Spitfire control column (the gun button safety catch) was found during that excavation thus pointing to a Spitfire VB or Mk IX . This find positively ruled out Bader's Spitfire VA, although Sergeant Donald Bostock's crash in the same vicinity could not, as yet, be ruled out as a possibility for this particular crash site as absolutely no evidence of the specific identity of this Spitfire could be found, either during the recovery or subsequent cleaning of the finds.

This Spitfire was ultimately identified by elimination as that flown by Jack Misseldine and the author was able to re-unite Jack with a part of his old Spitfire, the brass bezel from the cockpit clock, during July 2007.

Spitfire IX MA764, MT-L 122 Squadron, 25 November 1943, Flight Sergeant D Bostock
The circumstantial report of the commanding officer of 122 Squadron states:

Flight Sergeant D Bostock took off from Gravesend at 15.10hrs on 25 November 1943 as Blue three with ten other aircraft of 122 Squadron on a fighter sweep to the Lille area. Whilst over the Béthune area two Messerschmitt 109s joined the squadron mistaking the squadron for "friends", as the squadron also took them to be "friends". The squadron broke up, and one enemy aircraft was seen to fire from extreme range. Just after this, Flight Sergeant Bostock called up to say he had a high glycol temperature. I told him to try to glide home, but he was apparently already down to 10,000ft and pouring glycol. He was not seen or heard of again.

Like Jack Misseldine, Donald Bostock was also able to evade and return home to the UK. His M19 de-brief gave the outline of events:

At about 16.00hrs we were attacked by Me 109s. I was hit in the glycol pipe lead; my engine started to fail and caught fire and I was compelled to bale out.

I came down about five miles north of Aire in the grounds of a farmhouse. Several French people ran towards me. One of them made signs that he would look after my parachute, which had got caught in a tree, and my Mae West. Another indicated by signs that I was to follow him and we ran towards the farmhouse about sixty yards away. He hid me in a little outhouse and found me some civilian clothes, taking my uniform which he said he was going to burn. I asked if the Germans were in the neighbourhood, and he nodded, so I was taken down to a cellar and practically covered over with sacks of potatoes.

I heard a car draw up and some guttural German voices; a search was obviously taking place. A German soldier came to my cellar and looked about, but failed to discover me. I was in the cellar about two hours altogether.

When the Germans had gone the people fetched me out and took me back to the outhouse where I was given a meal. I spent the night in the outhouse but was unable to get much sleep owing to the cold. I could see that the people were afraid to keep me, so at dawn I set off and went across some fields and quite soon approached another farmhouse. Here I was taken in by a woman who was cooking something and allowed to warm myself. A young man gave me better civilian clothes and I understood from him that he would fetch a French lady that afternoon who could speak English.

At about 18.00hrs the lady turned up and told me that she knew a man who might be able to help me. That evening the man turned up and from this point on I was helped on my journey.

As with Jack Misseldine, Donald Bostock's journey was also an extraordinary one which ultimately resulted in his successful evasion from the Germans and his return to the UK on 17 January 1944.

From the information given by Madame Cappe, it certainly seemed likely that the Spitfire down in her field was Bostock's machine, although she was adamant that it had exploded and burnt on impact (her late husband had been ploughing the field at the time!) and what was left of the Spitfire was entirely taken away, she said, by the German salvage squads, the Bergungskomando. Nothing, she said, was left buried in the ground.

An excavation there in late 2005 proved this was not the case and that it was, indeed, Donald Bostock's Spitfire. By a process of elimination, therefore, the Spitfire alongside the road between Blaringhem and Sercus looked almost certain to have been the aeroplane abandoned by Misseldine. This pointed yet more convincingly to the crash at Mont Dupil as being Douglas Bader's aeroplane. There remained just one other Spitfire that needed to be ruled out, although the earlier Malvern Spitfire Team expedition had effectively already done this.*

Spitfire Mk IX LZ996 421 Squadron, 17 June 1943, Squadron Leader P L I Archer
This Spitfire was lost in combat with Focke-Wulf 190s in the St Omer region on 17 June 1943, its pilot killed. The crash site of a Spitfire had been located by the Malvern team near Boeseghem and the site subsequently excavated by them in the summer of 1996 in the belief that it was Bader's W3185. The recovery proved the aeroplane to have been a much later cannon-armed Spitfire Mk IX variant. No evidence was found positively to tie this wreckage to Squadron Leader Archer, although a wrist watch and a parachute "D"-ring were found in the remains of the cockpit. Clearly, the pilot had died in this crash and published links have continued to be made to Archer by those involved with the Malvern team right up until 2006.

In fact, records clearly show that Squadron Leader Archer was killed in Spitfire LZ966 when his aircraft crashed into a field at Alquines, west of Lumbres, some forty kilometres away from the excavated site near Boeseghem. Here, at Alquines, Marcel Wintrebert recalled the crash of a Spitfire which hit the top of a tall tree as it attempted to land and crashed heavily into an adjacent cabbage field. The pilot was killed, having suffered terrible facial injuries and a smashed leg. Marcel, then a young boy, recalled the crash was either June or July 1943 and also remembered seeing the pilot's identity card which showed him to be Canadian. The body, he said, was taken away to St Omer for burial. Given Wintrebert's clear recall, and the established facts of Archer's loss, it seems reasonable to assume that Spitfire crash at Alquines this involved Squadron Leader Archer.

Other than that, we also have the fact that the Spitfire excavated at Boeseghem was evidently a Mk IX variant with a Rolls-Royce Merlin 61 (reportedly numbered 82021/82075) whereas LZ996 was fitted with a Merlin 63 (number unknown) and had only been delivered to the RAF on 14 May 1943, a little over a month before its loss in action. In the intervening period of its service life its individual operational history rules out an engine change, even if one were to accept the unlikely possibility of LZ996 being "retro-fitted" with a Merlin 61. As to the engine numbers reportedly found by the Malvern team, both (if they are correct) are Merlin 61 numbers and the existence of two numbers is indicative of a rebuild involving two different engines. 82021 came off build on 15 June 1942. Records show that it was later overhauled and sent to Biggin Hill on 30 January 1943. Records also show that it was later "written off", but no date is given. Merlin 82075 came off build on 25 June 1942 and was last recorded on 10 February 1943 at 7 MU, RAF Quedgeley. It is not recorded as written off. However, it may be concluded that if 82021 and 82075 became a composite engine upon overhaul at some point, then the date of the Spitfire crash excavated at Boeseghem cannot have been before 30 January 1943 and was most probably later than 10 February 1943.

* For the duration of the hunt for Bader's Spitfire, and for the excavation of Bostock's and Misseldine's aeroplanes, the Wildfire TV crew and recovery/investigation team used the very same outhouse where Bostock had been hidden as their operational base, canteen, office and "command centre".

NB: The existence of an engine number alone is insufficient to apply an identity to the actual aircraft itself. The air ministry form 78 aircraft movement cards held on each individual airframe (essentially the aircraft's "logbook") usually record engine numbers fitted to that particular aircraft at time of delivery to the RAF from the factory. They do not usually record subsequent engine changes that would have inevitably occurred during the life of that aeroplane. Consequently, and if an aircraft had been lost before any engine changes had taken place, it might be possible to help confirm the actual aircraft serial number by linking the number of any discovered/recovered engine to that recorded on the AM form 78. A failure to be able to link that recorded engine number to any discovered/recovered engine does not necessarily rule out a specific airframe serial number. Equally, though, a confirmed match of engine serial numbers helps to strengthen the case for identification.

APPENDIX K

SPITFIRE W3185 – HISTORY

The history of all RAF airframes was recorded on the individual aircraft movement card, or air ministry form 78. The record card for W3185 shows the aeroplane to have been built by Vickers Armstrong under contract number 19773/39 as a Mk VA and fitted with a Rolls-Royce Merlin XLV. The engine number was not recorded on the card, and therefore any potential linking of an engine number to W3185 is impossible. The Spitfire's history in RAF service is shown below:

Taken on Charge at 39 MU, RAF Colerne – 11 May 1941
To 145 Squadron – 30 June 1941
To Air Service Training – 22 July 1941 (for minor adjustments)
To 145 Squadron – 22 July 1941
To 41 Squadron – 28 July 1941
To 616 Squadron – 28 July 1941
Flying Battle – Missing 9 August 1941
Struck off Charge – 17 August 1941
The total number of flying hours is not recorded.

On 14 July 1941, whilst serving with 145 Squadron in the Tangmere Wing, Squadron Leader P S "Stan" Turner claimed a Messerschmitt 109 as damaged south-west of Calais while flying W3185.

The Spitfire is shown on the AM form 78 to be a presentation aircraft named "Lord Lloyd". Other sources have stated the aeroplane to have been named "Lord Lloyd I", although this is not actually confirmed on the aeroplane's individual record card. Spitfire W3185 was purchased by Mr Oswald Finney of Alexandria as one of two Spitfires paid for in memory of Lord Lloyd, chairman of The British Council.

APPENDIX L
THE SAGA OF THE LEG

POST OFFICE TELEGRAM

Charges to pay		OFFICE STAMP
s. d.		NORTH FORELAND 13 AU 41 RADIO
RECEIVED		

Prefix. Time handed in. Office of Origin and Service Instructions. Words.

1134 m **4** (Confirmation copy)

From FFU   FFU   To

B

Northforelandradio de FFU

Wing Commander Douglas Bader am 9.8.41 in gefangenschaft geraten.
Beifallschirmabsprung prothese des rechten beines verloren.
Bader erbittet schnellste uebersendung neuer prothese.
Abwurf mit fallschirm von deutsher seite freigestellt.
Tag und uhr zeit des abwurfes auf funk weg uebermittelnat abwurfort abwurfort
wird dann von hier bezeichnet.
Abwurfflugzeug hat freies geleit.

For free repetition of doubtful words telephone "TELEGRAMS ENQUIRY" or call, with this form at office of delivery. Other enquiries should be accompanied by this form and, if possible, the envelope.

Wireless notification of Bader's capture and request for spare artificial leg.

The document reproduced above is the original telegram from North Foreland radio to HQ Fighter Command. The translation of the document is as follows:

Wing Commander Douglas Bader taken prisoner on 9 August 1941 lost his right leg while baling out. Bader requests that a new leg be sent. German permission granted to drop it by parachute. Communicate day and time of delivery by radio. Delivering aircraft will be granted safe conduct.

On 19 August 1941 the spare leg was duly delivered during the course of Circus 81, the operational order for which is set out below:

18 August 1941
OPERATION "LEG" (CIRCUS EIGHTY-ONE)
To take place a.m. Tuesday 19th August 1941

1. TARGET: For 6 Blenheims
   Power Station at Gosnay – 3½ miles SW of Béthune
   Bombing Height 10,000ft
2. RENDEZVOUS: At 10,000ft over Manston at 08.30hrs
3. ESCORT WING: Tangmere: At 11,000, 12,000 and 14,000ft
   41, 610, 616

The Blenheim of 18 Squadron (R3843) that delivered Bader's spare artificial leg.

4. ESCORT COVER WING: Kenley: At 15,000, 17,000 and 20,000ft
                                452, 485, 602 (Gain height N of Thames)

5. BOMBER ROUTES AND TIMINGS:

Manston	08.30
W of Gravelines	08.42
W of St Omer	08.47
Gosnay (Target)	08.53
Mardyck	09.06
Manston	09.21

6. TARGET SUPPORT WINGS:

    Northolt: At 22,000, 24,000 and 28,000ft
    303, 308, 315   (To gain height N of Thames)
    To rendezvous with bombers and accompany them to St Omer, then draw ahead to target if not engaged. Then to attain air superiority and follow bombers out.
    Hornchurch: At 28,000 to 32,000ft E of Dunkirk to Béthune. To arrive over Béthune 08.50hrs. Follow bombers out.

7. REAR SUPPORT WING:

    Biggin Hill
    72, 92, 609: 10 miles SE of Dunkirk at 28,000 to 32,000 ft, to be in position at 08.56hrs; to watch out especially for enemy aircraft coming from direction of Ostend. Follow main formation back at discretion of wing leader.

8. INFORMATION:

    The leg is to be dropped by a Blenheim when west of St Omer. The wing leader of the Tangmere Escort Wing is to report by R/T when the parachute has opened "LEG GONE". Tangmere controller is to report to group controller immediately he receives this message.

    (Sgd.) S F Vincent, Group Captain, Biggin Hill.

As the parachute billowed open above the leg box, the "LEG GONE" message was sent, resulting shortly afterwards in the following signal:

To: No. 2 Group and all stations
From: Headquarters No 11 Group
19/8/41
Circus 81
During this operation the leg for Wing Commander Bader became airborne at 10.51hrs and was last seen floating down gracefully SW of St Omer.
At 11.00hrs a message was broadcast to the enemy informing him that the leg had just been dropped by parachute. The message was acknowledged.
Preliminary reports indicate seven Me 109s destroyed

Three Me 109s probably destroyed

Five Me 109s damaged

For the loss of two of our pilots.
No bombs were dropped during this operation. All bombers returned safely*

The delivering aircraft was a Blenheim of 18 Squadron, R3843, WV-F, crewed by Sergeant J M Nickleson (RCAF), Sergeant W Meadows and Sergeant J Pearson. (These three crew members were lost and killed in the same aircraft, R3843, on 20 September 1941 when they flew into the bomb bursts of another aircraft attacking shipping off Zandvoort. Nickleson was never found and has no known grave. Meadows and Pearson were both buried in the Netherlands.)
The box with Bader's spare leg also included a letter as follows:

To: Commandant
Luftwaffe, St Omer (Longuenesse) Aerodrome
WING COMMANDER DOUGLAS BADER DSO DFC
Royal Air Force (prisoner of war).
1) The general broadcast message transmitted by you on 500 Kcs by Station Ushant at 11.35hrs (GMT) on August 13th 1941 in respect of Wing Commander Bader was received by me.
2) This box contains an artificial leg to replace the right leg this officer lost during his descent by parachute over France on the 9th August 1941.
3) Please accept my thanks, both for your broadcast message and anything you can do to ensure that this new leg is delivered to Wing Commander Bader as soon as possible.
August 1941. Air Vice-Marshal, Royal Air Force.**

Another letter, this time from Sergeant Jack Pearson of 18 Squadron to his mother, tells of his part in the delivery of the leg. It is reproduced here:

---

* In fact, intense flak was encountered and all six of the Blenheims committed to the operation were damaged, with one observer, Sergeant Lee, being seriously wounded in the thigh. More than two RAF fighter pilots were lost, with at least five Spitfires lost or damaged, and two pilots killed, one PoW, one wounded and one safe. The prisoner of war was Pilot Officer Anthony of 403 Squadron who had flown on Circus 68 and claimed one Me 109 as probably destroyed during that operation.
** This is Air Vice-Marshal Leigh-Mallory, although he is not named in person in the actual letter.

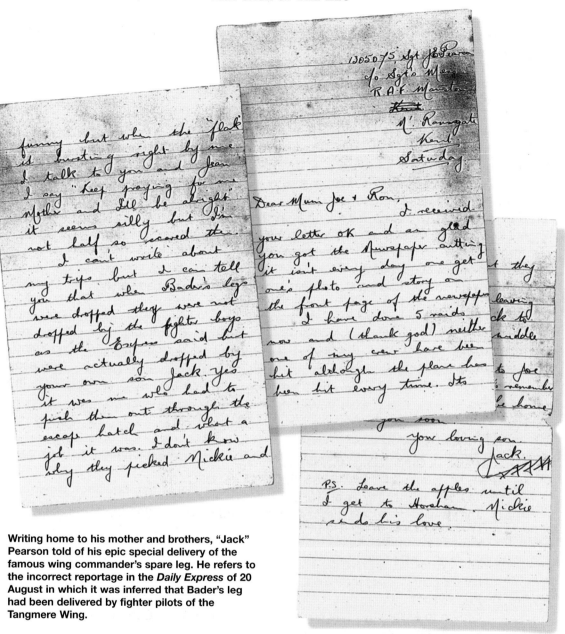

Writing home to his mother and brothers, "Jack" Pearson told of his epic special delivery of the famous wing commander's spare leg. He refers to the incorrect reportage in the *Daily Express* of 20 August in which it was inferred that Bader's leg had been delivered by fighter pilots of the Tangmere Wing.

With Bader at large in St Omer town on 19 August 1941 he actually heard and witnessed from the ground the proceedings of Circus 81 above him, unaware that the delivery of his spare leg was taking place!

Several post-war references to this drop have been made in a variety of different publications stating that this delivery comprised a spare set of both artificial legs. In fact, only one (the right leg) was delivered. Further, there is no evidence either that the box contained toilet requisites and tobacco along with a personal letter for Bader as has frequently been stated. The delivery, apparently at least, adhered wholly to the specifics of the German request, i.e. a spare right leg.

151

Appendix M

The Search for Bader

When the Tangmere wing leader failed to return from Circus 68 on 9 August 1941 a search was initiated by A Flight of 616 Squadron. The following Fighter Command signal gave these details:

To: HQ Fighter Command Intelligence

From: 11 Group Intelligence   IG/470   9/8/41

PATROL REPORT FROM HAWKINGE

Six Spitfire VBs of 616 Squadron took off from Westhampnett at 14.20hrs 9/8/41 headed by Flight Lieutenant Dundas to search for Wing Commander Bader who has not returned from Circus operations this morning. A sweep was made from Le Touquet to Gravelines. They did not sight any wreckage or dinghy. Flight Lieutenant Dundas reports that two small convoys protected by E boats were sighted, one convoy proceeding from Gravelines towards Calais with four E boats ahead and three or four ships of from 2,000 to 3,000 tons. The other convoy between Le Touquet and Cap Gris Nez of three ships (merchantmen) of 2,000 tons protected by four E boats. He also reports having sighted a submarine two to three miles off shore and travelling in a westerly direction between Calais and Cap Gris Nez. Pilot Officer Heppell fired a short burst at the submarine periscope which was visible but without observing any results. Flight Lieutenant Dundas reports that they received fairly accurate flak from the E boats which were protecting the convoy proceeding from Gravelines to Calais.

Six aircraft landed at Hawkinge at 15.30hrs.

The six aircraft then departed Hawkinge and arrived back at Westhampnett thirty minutes later.

Although it is, of course, inconceivable that these six pilots of 616 Squadron would not also be searching for any other pilot down in the Channel it is interesting to note that such was the perceived importance of the man to RAF Fighter Command, this was specifically described as a search for Bader. No mention is made of the missing 616 Squadron B Flight commander, Casson, who might equally have been in the sea along with his wing leader.

APPENDIX N

AIR INTELLIGENCE (AIk) REPORT 398/1941

Interrogation of prisoner of war Hauptmann Rolf Pingel, I/JG 26.

On 10 July 1941 Hauptmann Rolf Pingel, the commander of I Gruppe JG 26, was shot down and taken PoW at St Margaret's Bay, Kent. He made a perfect wheels-up forced landing in his Me 109 F, thus delivering to the RAF its first example of this variant of the Messerschmitt 109. Not only were the RAF able to fully evaluate this "prize" in the air after it had been repaired, but intelligence gleaned from Pingel's interrogation was extremely valuable. Additionally, what he told his interrogators places a valuable contemporary insight into the Luftwaffe perspective of the situation in the air over northern France during the summer of 1941.

Hauptmann Rolf Pingel.

A great deal of the preamble of report 398/1941 has no great relevance in the overall picture of the Luftwaffe/RAF situation of that period, but the main body of his interrogation summary contains much of interest:

Daylight Raids
- This Prisoner of War was very pleased that the English have at last decided to go over to France. This reverses the position of last September, and the Germans are able to save a large number of their pilots.
- He maintained that the British losses during the three weeks preceeding 10 July 1941 had been nearly one hundred, and the German losses in pilots between one fifth and one third of that amount.
- He also maintained that the British claims for this period (one hundred and twenty five German aircraft) must be incorrect because this would represent the wiping out of half the available fighter strength and they could not possibly have replaced this number.
- During the three weeks period, I/JG 26 had lost eight pilots killed and claimed to have brought down no fewer than sixty English aircraft.
- The figures of British losses published in our communiqués are popularly thought to be completely inaccurate since we "do not count losses of Czech or Polish pilots".
- The opinion was expressed that it would be a mistake for the Germans to reinforce their fighter strength on the Western front. The comparatively weak opposition at the moment is a temptation for the British to come over and thus lose pilots.

- In this way the RAF will be weakened ready for the final German offensive which will follow the successful conclusion of the Soviet war.
- The bombs dropped during these raids, though damage was admitted, did not seriously worry the Germans. The operations had, however, one most valuable result in that they were a source of very great satisfaction for the French.

Me 109 F

- This pilot believes the Me 109 F to be superior in every respect to the Spitfire, except that the new Spitfire might, when handled by an equally good pilot, still be superior to the Me 109 F in steep turns at high speed. The difference, however, can be more than counter balanced if the German pilot is better.
- The re-designed wing of the Me 109 F considerably improves the handling of the aircraft and the slots open more gradually so that turns are very much easier to execute.
- The controls are, however, still fairly stiff at high speed and particularly as the cockpit is fairly cramped fighter pilots are at an advantage if powerfully built.
- The outstanding disadvantage of the Me 109 F is that the wings are not as stable as they might be. At least two pilots, including the redoubtable Hauptmann Balthasar, (see page 89) kommodore of the Richthofen Geschwader, have been killed within the last three weeks by tearing the wings off their Me 109s when trying to follow Spitfires in a snaking dive. After a fast dive pilots have to pull out fairly gradually.
- The rated altitude of the Me 109 F is probably in the neighbourhood of 20,000ft and the speed at that height is said to be 620 kph (384mph)
- The combat ceiling is 34,000ft and the all-out ceiling 39,600ft. The manoeuvrability between the rated altitude and the combat ceiling falls away equally with that of the Spitfire and therefore the comparative handling of the two aircraft will be similar at all heights.
- The endurance, as expressed by the range on which sorties are based, is 60/65 minutes. So far the Me 109 Fs have not been fitted with extra tanks but this is a future development which is to be expected.
- The 2cm MG151 with which this particular aircraft was armed was fitted at this pilot's own request (sic) because it has the same high muzzle velocity as the standard MG151 and the damage caused by the 2cm shell would be greater.
- The standard MG151 is well liked once the pilot has learned to aim high. A big advantage with this gun is that jams can be cleared from the cockpit.
- The new arrangement of the guns in the nose of the Me 109 F enables pilots to fire very accurately while in a turn and to open fire at a greater range. This pilot, however, usually opened fire at about one hundred yards, closing to fifty yards. There have been absolutely no unfavourable comments on the reduction of the armament; the present arrangement is regarded as ideal.
- The Me 109 F does not appear yet to have been fitted with any gadgets for simulating damage, although this is a development about which there has been considerable talk, particularly as a Spitfire which made a belly landing in France two weeks ago was rumoured to have been fitted with an apparatus for producing white smoke.
- The black smoke sometimes seen to issue from the Me 109 F is probably due to full boost and the white smoke, if this is not condensation, is quite possibly due to a hit in the radiator.

German Fighter Tactics
- Owing to the fact that the German fighter pilots are having to re-orientate themselves from offensive to defensive warfare, German fighter tactics are at the moment still in a state of re-adjustment.
- One of the main changes that has taken place is that fighter aircraft are now controlled from the ground.
- This was at first a source of some discontent to the fighter pilots who were accustomed to act much more on their own initiative, but it has been found that the ground control is working quite efficiently and usually gets the fighters to their prey in time.
- The British reporting service is, however, considered to be superior. It is even stated that if ground control do not know where their own aircraft are they tune into British R/T to find out.
- The efficiency and devotion to duty of the British close escort was very highly praised, and unfavourable comparisons were drawn between the English and German fighter pilots in this respect.
- The ground control is very insistent that only the British bombers shall be attacked and for this reason this pilot, when leading the gruppe, has on at least ten occasions during the last three weeks refrained from attacking fighters even though at a tactical advantage.
- Of late, the British close escort has become so efficient that the only way to get at the bombers is to approach from behind and above and dive through the formation at full throttle.
- When attacked by a single Spitfire this pilot's usual evasive action was to do a half-roll and dive away. This is possibly a well known part of evasive action. The dive, though steep, would not be vertical because of the danger of straining the wings.
- After pulling out of the dive, it was claimed that the Me 109 F could, in the hands of a good pilot, do four complete rolls on the climb before having to level off.
- Actually, this pilot was of the opinion that fighter tactics should continually be changing, and I/JG 26 always try to work a continual succession of ideas.
- The Stirling is considered a formidable opponent for a fighter, as it is well able to look after itself. It was described as pouring fire from every orifice.

British Tactics
- The more open formations recently adopted by British fighters were regarded as being obviously superior to their previous tactics because each pilot has a better vision and is thus able to defend himself and the others.
- Individual British fighter pilots were highly and sincerely praised. Even the new pilots seemed to have learned a lot very quickly.
- The original Spitfire carrying eight machine guns was unpleasant enough, but the new Spitfire V really impressed this man when he saw a Me 109 burst into pieces in mid-air over St Omer after a single short burst of fire.
- One of the most worrying features of British tactics was the continual changing of the height and direction of approach, so that the defence never knew where to expect the next attack.

Officers of JG 26
- Oberstleutnant Galland still leads the geschwader and has the full confidence of his subordinates who regard him firstly as an organisational genius and secondly as a brilliant airman.
- His claim to seventy-two victories is sincerely believed, but his habit of chain-smoking cigars is deplored.

Interrogation
- It has been possible to obtain a fairly accurate picture of German interrogation methods, although full details could not be obtained because even an officer with the standing of gruppen kommandeur is not fully in the know.
- Any unwounded prisoner captured is taken immediately to an aerodrome where he becomes the guest of selected members of the mess. Sometimes an army officer, but more usually a Luftwaffe intelligence officer in the uniform of the flying personnel arrives and joins the party which is being held in honour of the prisoner. He usually joins the party after it has been going on for some time and champagne and conversation are flowing.
- The choice of this officer is made by the IC (intelligence officer) of the Fliegerkorps, and it is he who attends to the interrogation, requirements, escort and movement of the prisoner.
- This treatment may be continued for as much as two days before this man is sent elsewhere.

Signed: Wing Commander S D Felkin, AI1(k) 20 July 1941

This report on the interrogation of Rolf Pingel gives a fascinating and very illuminating insight into many aspects of Luftwaffe operations by JG 26 and in the Pas de Calais area generally, not least of all the fact that Bader's "entertainment" in the mess at Audembert was a far from unique event and cannot be attributed merely to the hospitality of his hosts or his celebrity status. Details about German tactics, claims, losses, British tactics, the aircraft used and Luftwaffe interrogation methods are all highly relevant within the context of this book coming as they did from one of Galland's gruppe commanders and so close in time to the actual date of Circus 68.

In Memoriam
The Casualties of Circus 68

SELECTED BIBLIOGRAPHY

The following books and publications were amongst those referred to by the author during the preparation of this work.

Baker, David: *Adolf Galland – The Authorised Biography* (Windrow & Greene, 1996)

Boot, Henry & Sturtivant, Ray: *Gifts of War* (Air Britain, 2005)

Brickhill, Paul: *Reach for the Sky* (Collins, 1954)

Brown, Peter Sqn Ldr AFC: *Honour Restored* (Spellmount, 2005)

Caldwell, Donald L: *The JG 26 War Diary* (Grub Street, 1996)

Caldwell, Donald L: *JG 26 Photographic History of the Luftwaffe Top Guns* (Airlife, 1994)

Cross, ACM Sir Kenneth "Bing" & Prof Orange, Vincent: *Straight & Level* (Grub Street, 1993)

Deere, Gp Capt Alan C, DSO, OBE, DFC: *Nine Lives* (Hodder & Stoughton, 1959)

Dundas, Hugh: *Flying Start* (Stanley Paul, 1988)

Foreman, John: *1941: The Turning Point* (Air Research Publications, 1993)

Foreman, John: *RAF Fighter Command Victory Claims* (Part Two) (Red Kite, 2005)

Franks, Norman L R: *RAF Fighter Command Losses 1939-41* (Midland Publishing, 1997)

Galland, Adolf: *The First and the Last* (Franz Schneekluth, 1953)

Gretzyngier, Robert: *Poles in Defence of Britain* (Grub Street, 2001)

Haugland, Vern: *The Eagle Squadrons* (David & Charles, 1979)

Holmes, Tony: *American Eagles* (Classic Publications, 2001)

Johnson, Johnnie: *Wing Leader* (Chatto & Windus, 1956)

Kent, Gp Capt J A: *One of The Few* (William Kimber, 1971)

Lucas, Laddie: *Flying Colours* (Stanley Paul, 1981)

Matusiak, Wojtek: *Supermarine Spitfire I/II* (Stratus, 2007)

Obermaier, Ernst: *Die Ritterkeuztrager der Luftwaffe 1939-45* (Verlag Dieter Hoffmann, 1966)

Prien, Jochen: *Die Jagdfliegerverbande der Deutschen Luftwaffe 1939 bis 1945* (Teil 5) (Struve-Druck, 2003)

Priller, Josef: *JG 26 – Geschicte Eines Jagdgeschwaders* (Motor Buch Verlag, 1980)

Ramsey, Winston: *After The Battle Magazine No 35 & No 125*

Shores, Christopher & Williams, Clive: *Aces High* (Grub Street, 1994)

Shores, Christopher: *Aces High – Vol 2* (Grub Street, 1999)

Shores, Christopher: *Those Other Eagles* (Grub Street, 2004)

Slizewski, Grzegorz: *The Lost Hopes* (Panda, 2000)

Southall, Ivan: *Bluey Truscott* (Rainbow Publishing, 1989)

Stokes, Doug: *Paddy Finucane: Fighter Ace* (William Kimber, 1983)

Stokes, Doug: *Wings Aflame* (William Kimber, 1985)

Wynn, Kenneth G: *Men of The Battle of Britain* (CCB, 1999)

Zieliński, Józef: *Polish Airmen in The Battle of Britain* (Oficyna Wydawnicza, 2000)

INDEX